P...
TH...
THIN...   ...OOK

"The Creative Thinking Book *carries a fundamental message: we can all be innovators! It is in our DNA to be creative. This message should gladden the heart of any educator. At the same time, it is a call to action to all of us devoting our life to educating future generations – mothers, teachers, coaches, professors... creativity is contagious... cherish your creative potential and pass it along!"*

DR SUE ROSSANO-RIVERO
Acting Professor for Innovation Management and Business Development, FH Münster Universtity of Applied Sciences, Germany

"Neil and I grew up together, and he was my first ally as I began my own efforts at social innovation. His enthusiasm and curiosity are boundless, and here he communicates the joy and value to our humanity we can discover if we value creativity. This book is stuffed with inspiring stories and practical ways to unlock our imaginations."

DR SIMON DUFFY
President of Citizen Network

FOR OTHER TITLES
IN THE SERIES...

CONCISE
ADVICE
LAB

SMALL
BOOKS:
BIG
IDEAS

CLEVER CONTENT, DYNAMIC IDEAS, PRACTICAL
SOLUTIONS AND ENGAGING VISUALS –
A CATALYST TO INSPIRE NEW WAYS OF THINKING
AND PROBLEM-SOLVING IN A COMPLEX WORLD

conciseadvicelab.com

Published by
LID Publishing
An imprint of LID Business Media Ltd.
LABS House, 15-19 Bloomsbury Way,
London, WC1A 2TH, UK

info@lidpublishing.com
www.lidpublishing.com

A member of:

BPR ✹

businesspublishersroundtable.com

© Neil Francis, 2022
© LID Business Media Limited, 2022

Printed by Imak Ofset

ISBN: 978-1-911671-44-2
ISBN: 978-1-911671-45-9 (ebook)

Cover and page design: Caroline Li

THE CREATIVE THINKING BOOK

HOW TO IGNITE AND BOOST YOUR CREATIVITY

NEIL FRANCIS

MADRID | MEXICO CITY | LONDON
BUENOS AIRES | BOGOTA | SHANGHAI

To Jack, Lucy and Sam

With loads of love

TO START, A STORY TO GET YOU IN THE RIGHT MOOD FOR MY BOOK

One day, a professor entered his classroom and asked his students to prepare for a surprise test. They all waited anxiously at their desks for the exam to begin.

The professor handed out the exams with the text facing down, as usual. Once he'd distributed them, he asked the students to turn over the papers.

To everyone's surprise, there were no questions — just a black dot in the centre of the paper. The professor, seeing the expression on everyone's faces, told them the following: "I want you to write about what you see there." The students, confused, got started on the inexplicable task.

At the end of the class, the professor collected the exams and started reading them out loud in front of the students.

All of them, without exception, defined the black dot, trying to explain its position in the centre of the sheet. After all had been read, the classroom fell silent, and the professor started to explain:

"I'm not going to grade you on this, I just wanted to give you something to think about. No one wrote about the white part of the paper.

Everyone focused on the black dot, and the same thing happens in our lives."

His message was that we tend to ignore so many things around us, or don't see them to begin with, even though they are right in front of our noses. They are things that would inspire you, from observing a beautiful butterfly in flight to watching the waves on a beach as they crash into rocks. All around you is a world packed with wonderful things that could light the touch paper that would unlock your mind, where you'd discover an exciting new world you never knew existed.

However, if you insist on focusing only on the black dot – wanting that new car, envious of a neighbour's holiday plans, constantly working through the weekend rather than spending time with your family, focused on which 48-inch TV you should purchase – all you will do is focus on the black dots. The white expanse, with all the possibilities it offers, will be invisible.

Take your eyes away from the black dots in your lives.

Find where the open, unexplored white parts are, and you'll find the space where creative solutions to your problems and challenges will present themselves.

Understanding the power of creativity is the most exciting thing you can discover in your life.

CONTENTS

ACKNOWLEDGMENTS

A massive thank you to:

Martin Liu, Aiyana Curtis and Brian Doyle
at the brilliant LID Publishing.

All the people that appear in the book which
inspired me to share their stories.

My wife, Louise, for doing the first draft edits
and still staying calm!

And for my two daft Golden Retrievers,
Archie and Harris, whose long walks on the beaches
of North Berwick provided me the perfect space
and environment to plan the book.

INTRODUCTION
ALBANY STREET

In the mid-1990s, two businesses were started in Albany Street, in the New Town area of Edinburgh, Scotland.

At 20 Albany Street, the web development agency called Company Net started trading. I was the co-founder and CEO.

At 14 Albany Street, the Scottish edition of *The Big Issue* — the street magazine that offers homeless people and those at risk an opportunity to earn a legitimate income — had already begun publishing. It was established by social activist Mel Young, who was inspired by the success of *The Big Issue* in England and its 1990s forerunner, *Street News*, in New York City.

Today, *The Big Issue* is the world's most widely circulated street magazine, and its Scottish edition has been a huge success.

Setting up shop just 80 feet away from one another, Mel and I got to know each other, and we've kept in touch over the last 25 years. I have always greatly admired Mel and his work as a dedicated and creative social entrepreneur. He has a passion for social justice, especially around homelessness.

In 2001, in a Cape Town bar, Mel found himself chatting with Harald Schmied, founder of an Austrian street paper. They discussed other ways they could help the homeless, and over a few beers the creative juices started to flow. It seems that they both loved the game of football, and that was the creative spark that led them to set up a football tournament for the homeless. Even better they thought, if FIFA can have a World Cup for professional footballers, then why could they not set up a World Cup for the homeless?

Within two years, the first Homeless World Cup was held in Graz, Austria. It is now an annual football tournament, featuring men's and women's teams, organized by the Homeless World Cup Foundation, which advocates for the end of homelessness through football. Each year, the foundation's network of street football partners selects more than 500 players to compete in the event. These partners operate in more than 450 locations, reaching 100,000 homeless people each year.

To date, the Homeless World Cup Foundation and its partners have impacted the lives of 1.2 million homeless people around the globe. Mel is the current president of the organization.

I recently met with Mel to catch up over coffee. He explained that while the tournament had to be cancelled over the last few years because of the coronavirus epidemic, plans were proceeding for the 20th Homeless World Cup to be staged in September 2022, in New York City.

I asked if he ever could have imagined, in that bar in Cape Town 21 years ago, that the event would turn out to be a global success that touched the lives of more than a million people.

"Absolutely not," he laughed. "But I guess that if you identify a need to solve a new or difficult problem, such as changing the lives of the homeless, and you're determined to achieve that, then anything is possible. Obviously, in that bar, the atmosphere was perfect for being creative and inventive. That allowed us to link the two things that we were both passionate about, football and helping the homeless, and come up a new solution – The Homeless World Cup."

He said, "I guess this shows that the power of being creative is to come up with solutions. And from there, you have no idea where that journey will end."

Inspired by the creative thinking that has had such a positive effect on homeless people worldwide, I set out to try and create the right 'atmosphere' in a new book that would help people become more creative in their thinking. I can't guarantee that you will see the same world-changing results, but you never know!

First, a few definitions. I see Creative Thinking as a way of looking at problems or situations from a fresh perspective, leading to the conception of something original. This leads to Inventive Thinking, where that 'something new' is actually created. If you have a brainstorming session and dream up dozens of new ideas, you have displayed creativity, but there is no actual inventiveness until something gets implemented. The idea of an international sporting event to help the homeless was a creative one indeed.

Inventiveness happens when things start to be implemented using your creativity, imagination and knowledge. This could be a concept, a solution, a method or an actual physical thing. In other words, whenever you physically try to do something new, it turns into an act of invention. The idea of The Homeless World Cup moved from being a creative thought to an inventive one when Mel and Harold moved forward with making the event a reality.

It all starts with firing up your imagination — conceptualizing novel ideas, images or notions in the mind without any immediate input from the senses. Every creative thought starts with your imagination, and it is your imagination that then leads you to be inventive.

So, creativity and inventiveness go together hand in hand, and throughout this book I will use the words inventive, inventiveness, creative and creativity.

It's time to become more creative, as it is in your DNA!

"

Imagination is more important than knowledge.

"

Albert Einstein

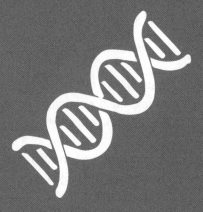

PART ONE

WE WERE BORN TO BE CREATIVE

FROM MARCUS
TO HESTON
IN OUR DNA

In the sleepy countryside village of Bray, about an hour's drive from London, the gastronomic world was turned on its head in 1995 with the arrival of The Fat Duck restaurant.

The owner and head chef, Heston Blumenthal, was to revolutionize restaurant menus. He was an early adopter of *sous vide* cooking ('under vacuum' in French), which involves sealing food in a bag with seasonings and sauces and slow-cooking it in a precisely temperature-controlled water bath. This gradual, controlled cooking technique produces dishes of unparalleled flavour, texture, aroma and visual appeal.

Additionally, Blumenthal's was first restaurant to harness the culinary potential of liquid nitrogen. Because the liquefied gas is so incredibly cold (-196 degrees Celsius; -320 degrees Fahrenheit), it is used to instantaneously freeze foods, forming microscopic ice crystals that yield an unbelievably creamy consistency.

With these and other 'molecular gastronomy' techniques, Blumenthal developed extraordinary creations like snail porridge, bacon and egg ice cream, and the lauded triple-cooked chips. Dishes are served with additional sensory inputs, such as 'Sounds of the Sea,' a plate of seafood served with a seafood foam on top of a 'beach' of tapioca sand, breadcrumbs and eel. Alongside this fanciful dish — featured in a 14-course tasting menu — diners are given an iPod to listen to crashing waves while they eat.

The Fat Duck, with Blumenthal at its helm, was hailed as a global game-changer. It has been called "a temple to innovative modern British cuisine," awarded a procession of Michelin stars and was in 2005 voted The World's Best Restaurant.

Now let's go back to the 1st century AD and Marcus Gavius Apicius, a Roman gourmet and lover of luxury, who contributed to one of the most famous ancient cookbooks, *De Re Coquinaria*. It contains hundreds of recipes, many of which are the earliest examples of their kind. There are chapters packed with detailed preparations for venison, gazelle, wild sheep, beef and veal, kid and lamb, pig, hare and dormouse.

It tells you a lot about Roman cooking, particularly for the wealthy classes, referencing exotic ingredients and complex methodologies. For instance, Apicius lays out two ways of cooking boar and seven different sauces to serve with it. Here is one aromatic accompaniment for your oven-roasted boar:

> *"Crush pepper, lovage, oregano, seedless myrtle berries, coriander and onions. Add honey, wine, broth and a little oil. Heat and tie together with roux. The boar, roasted in the oven, is masked with this sauce, which you may use for any kind of roast game."*

But what really struck me in reading these ancient recipes was that even with nearly 2,000 years separating Apicius and The Fat Duck's Blumenthal, both were pushing the boundaries of what adventurous cooking could be. They wanted their audiences to experience exciting new sensual delights. They saw their creations as a form of art.

It seems that inventiveness and creativity were baked into their DNA.

IT IS IN YOUR DNA?

Since the evolution of *Homo sapiens* — modern man — our world has been driven by flashes of inspiration. Civilization has evolved and progressed, driven by the process of creativity. The enduring question has always been whether the defining factors come from nature or nurture. Could it be that creativity literally resides in our DNA?

Potentially, yes.

In 1869, the English explorer and anthropologist Francis Galton, a relative of Charles Darwin, wrote a book on what he called "hereditary genius." Galton felt that the ability to come up with great ideas was passed down through generations.

A century and a half later — as recently as the early 2000s — we've continued to uncover new things about the brain and creativity. In fact, a number of recent studies seem to validate Galton's theory of genetic inheritance.

In 2009, a team from Cornell University's Department of Neurology and Neuroscience discovered that the brains of artistically creative individuals have a particular characteristic that may enhance imagination and inventiveness.

They found that the size of the corpus callosum, a bundle of more than 200 million nerve fibres that link the hemispheres of our brain, plays a crucial part in an individual's ability to think "divergently." Basically, the smaller this juncture was, the easier it was for the individual to be creative. It seems that a decrease in the connectivity between the right and left lobes allows each hemisphere to specialize, so ideas can develop more freely and fully. Writers, artists, musicians and other creative types were in fact found to have a smaller corpus callosum than others in the general population.

However, this does not tell the full story. Creativity is not only about divergent thinking, but also generating endless associations. Recent findings suggest that the secret to this lies in our DNA.

In 2013, researchers at Helsinki University looked at human genes and their relation to hereditary genius. Their study found that an individual's ability to be creative musically is linked to a particular cluster of genes known to be involved in the plasticity of the brain – its ability to reorganize itself by breaking and forming new connections between cells. The more plasticity your brain exhibits, the more creative you become.

This would seem to indicate that some people are inherently more creative than others. The key word here is the notion of 'more.' Everyone is creative; it is in our DNA. But we've been taught the myth that a lot of us are not creative because we were born to use mainly one side of our brain – the left side.

KILLING THE MYTH

Let's looks at this further. The right side of the brain, is associated with things like creativity, imagination and intuition, while the left side is associated with things like planning, logic and rationality. The argument goes that 'left-brain people' are more logical in their thinking, rather than imaginative, and simply cannot be all that creative.

That's a long-held belief... but science tells us it's simply not the case.

The brain's right hemisphere is not a separate organ, working in isolation from the left hemisphere. It is also incorrect to say that the left brain is uncreative.

The link between creativity and the right brain is pretty clear. The specialized characteristics of the right hemisphere make it the seat of curiosity, synergy, experimentation, metaphorical thinking, playfulness, solution finding, artistry, flexibility, synthesizing and risk taking. In addition, it is likely to be opportunistic, future oriented, welcoming of change and to function as the centre of our visualization capability.

Every one of these specialized modes is capable of enhancing an individual's creative thinking. For example, an intuitive idea that pops into your mind and appears to solve a problem can be experimented with, visualized, integrated with other ideas and ultimately developed into a possible solution. That's the right hemisphere part.

Now, to do something about that possible solution requires different specialized mental processes, and these, by and large, are located in the left hemisphere. Assessing the proposed solution to determine whether it represents a viable solution to the real problem makes use of our rational processes of analysis and logic.

The role of the right hemisphere is essential to the creative process. But it supplies only a half of the thinking needed to realize the full creative process. We also need the left hemisphere and both halves of the limbic system to optimize creative output. This is where we start to be come inventive: when we begin translating these creative thoughts into action.

Creativity is a whole-brain process. Kill the myth – which many are told from a young age, and believe and live their lives by – that they are just not creative people. While factors such as environment and upbringing play a crucial role in your brain's development, work done by scientists in Scandinavia and the US has shown that having the right genetic makeup can make your brain more inclined towards creative thinking. Having said that, every one of us, every day, uses creative thinking. You probably don't realize it.

YOU ARE A CREATIVE HUMAN BEING
Creativity is possible in all areas of human life. It can be evident in science, the arts, mathematics, technology, cuisine, teaching, politics, business... you name it. And, like many human capacities, our creative powers can be developed, cultivated and refined. Doing that involves an increasing mastery of awareness, skills, knowledge and ideas.

"

There is no doubt
that creativity is
the most important
human resource of all.
Without creativity,
there would be no
progress, and we would
be forever repeating
the same patterns.

"

Edward de Bono

Creativity is about fresh thinking that involves making critical judgments about whether what you're working on is any good, be it a theorem, a product design or a poem. Creative work typically passes through a series of phases. Sometimes, what you end up with is not what you had in mind when you started. Being creative is not just about having off-the-wall ideas and letting your imagination run free. It may involve all of that, but it also includes refining, testing and focusing on what you're doing. It's about blue-sky inspiration and original thinking, but also about critically judging whether the work in process is taking the right shape and is worthwhile, at least for the person producing it. It is about the right and left sides of your brain – the imaginative half and the rational half – working in partnership.

Creativity is not the opposite of discipline and control. On the contrary, creativity in any field may involve deep factual knowledge and high levels of practical skill. And creativity isn't a linear process in which you have to learn all the necessary skills before you get started. The real driver of creativity is an appetite for discovery and a passion to create fantastic new things that will enhance your life and the lives of those around you.

Going back to Marcus Gavius Apicius and Heston Blumenthal, both used creative thinking to produce wonderfully innovative food. But to do that, they also needed discipline, focus and logical thinking. Creativity is a mixture of all these things, where you have great ideas and the courage to 'go there,' but you also have to dedicate the necessary time, put in the hard work, learn by experience and strive to continually innovate and do things better.

Don't let anyone tell you that you aren't creative. You are. Now, it is is time to embrace the fact that it is also in your nature.

And with that, it's time to meet a Colombian archaeologist and anthropologist.

THE JAGUAR MEN
IN OUR NATURE

Let me introduce you to Carlos Castaño-Uribe, a Colombian archaeologist and anthropologist. In the 1980s, Carlos was abseiling down one of the peaks of Chiribiquete, a series of tabletop mountains in the Amazon rainforest, when he made a startling discovery.

"Hanging 300 metres up the rock face, I arrived at a vast stone ledge and found myself face to face with a pair of jaguars," he says. "They're painted looking at each other, though I felt in that moment that they were looking straight at me. I nearly fell off."

Since that startling meeting with the painted jungle cats, Carlos and his team have discovered more than 75,000 ancient cave and rock paintings, the largest concentration of rock art anywhere in the world. Some are 20,000 years old.

The density, size and positioning of the paintings — often high up on cliff faces — are unparalleled, and Carlos believes there are many more works to uncover. The mountain range was declared a UNESCO World Heritage Site in 2018, and is part of Colombia's largest national park, which covers 17,000 square miles. More than 80% of the mountains remain unexplored by archaeologists.

The paintings document the lives of ancient nomadic hunter-gatherers, showing in unusual detail their hunts, battles, dances and rituals, and a knowledge of plants and animals that suggests a sophisticated understanding of Amazon ecology.

"This makes Chiribiquete one of the few depictions of megafauna by a human hand in the entire world," says Dr Alexander Geurds, a professor at the University of Oxford's School of Archaeology.

By far the most commonly painted animal is the jungle's fiercest predator, the jaguar. Nearly a quarter of the images feature the animal, which played a key role in the religion of the group, now known as the Jaguar Men. Other images discovered by Carlos and his team depict long-extinct creatures such as megatheres — 20-foot, four-tonne ground sloths that died out about 10,000 years ago.

"It's the Rosetta Stone of the Americas," says Carlos, referring to the inscribed ancient granite stone that was key to deciphering Egyptian hieroglyphics. "Chiribiquete allows us to interpret the cave art of the whole Neotropical region, the oldest history of the continent."

My guess is that most of us thought that 'art' really started in the 16th and 17th centuries. Those were the days of were the days of Michelangelo, Titian and Rembrandt, who paved the way for Constable, Cezanne, Monet and Van Gough in the 1800s, and the modern art stars Picasso, Moore, Marhol, O'Keeffe, Emin and Banksy. But that notion is dashed when you look at the art of the Jaguar Men — it's thousands of years old.

Or you can go back further. One of the oldest examples of Sub-Saharan African art, the Blombos Cave rock art, consists of two pieces of rock engraved with abstract geometric crosshatching and a series of beads made from sea snail shells. They were discovered in 2002 and have been dated to around 70,000 BC. Then, there's the Venus of Tan-Tan, which dates to 200,000–500,000 BC and is said to be the earliest representation of the human form. The small quartzite carving was discovered in 1999 on the banks of the River Draa in Morocco.

Every civilization, in every part of the world where man has lived since *Homo sapiens* first walked the earth, has produced art. The question is, why? It is obviously an important means of communication; if had not proved so useful, our early ancestors would have stopped using it. As highlighted in the first chapter, creativity is in our DNA, and the Jaguar Men, the Blombos Cave art and the Venus of Tan-Tan lend that credence.

That all shows *how* we used art to convey information about ancestry and other culturally and spiritually important topics. But *why* are humans are so creative – driven to create something out of nothing – and therefore want make art?

WHERE DOES THIS COME FROM?

One area of the human experience that seems not to have parallels out in nature is the arts. Indeed, only a few animal species exhibit even the faintest hints of creative artistry.

There is an Indian artist named Siri, whose drawings — ranging from abstract works to representational landscapes and self-portraits — have sold for thousands of dollars. As described in many articles and broadcast pieces, she trained for many years, and can now dash off a painting in mere minutes.

Siri is a 50-year-old Asian Elephant.

Species closer to us, like orangutans, chimpanzee and gorillas, have all been taught to draw and paint. Like Siri, some have proved to be quite good at it. But they don't do it proactively. In every instance, people have prompted them to do so, while man himself has always made art. When our early ancestors looked up at the cave wall, dimly lit by a dying fire, they saw a canvas.

Imagination is the beginning of creation. You imagine what you desire, you will what you imagine, and at last, you create what you will.

George Bernard Shaw

But why? It is in fact our nature; creativity is big part of being human. It provides us with beauty that can inspire, protects and keeps us safe, helps us recall past events or emotions, brings us together, and aids in communication and education.

In an excellent article entitled 'Why Do Humans Make Art?' from Nathan Lents, Professor of Biology at the City University of New York, he list a number of reasons:

EXPRESSION OF BEAUTY

If you look back in history, humans have produced art for one simple reason – it is an expression of beauty. Regardless of how you define beauty, I suggest that nature and art are both inherently beautiful. Admiring a famous painting, listening to fantastic piece of music or a stunning sculpture can inspire, emotionally move us, and provides total relaxation as we live in the moment.

But art is very subjective, as what one person thinks is beautiful, another sees no beauty. However, universally, everyone will find art that will dazzle and take our breath away. This provides either a visual or audio stimulus that makes us feel alive. Art makes us human.

A TOOL FOR SURVIVAL

As humans evolved, so too did the ability to share valuable information which helped them to survive. Think of stories told around the campfire about the man who escaped the bear, or the woman who found a leaf to cure stomach sickness. These stories could also be communicated through song, dance, drawing and painting.

RECALL OF PAST EVENTS OR EMOTIONS

The hunting and gathering way of life common among our early ancestors required extensive visual memory. How else could they have accomplished the fashioning of simple tools, deciphered the migratory patterns of big game on the African savannah and organized effectively coordinated group hunting? These complicated skills require the comparison of current visual cues with past experience in a computational, predictive, replicable way.

Further still, the ability to make and use tools, a skill that began in apes and exploded in humans, requires a great deal of visual and tactile memory. It would be common sense to 'paint' this thing down for other members of the tribe.

AIDS COMMUNICATION AND EDUCATION

As language was developing in humans, it allowed us to begin teaching each other about the tools they'd made, the food they found, the dangers they encountered and the skills they'd perfected, whether they were just crude drawings made by dragging sticks in the dirt, or more elaborate drawings on stone 'canvases.' Again, the key feature was the ability to use visual representations to induce memory recall or visual understanding, allowing another human to comprehend and remember something.

Though we may differ in our understanding of certain art forms, there is no question that creativity that leads to art is part of every culture and community around the globe. People have been creating music, dancing, painting, drawing, telling stories and bringing all these art forms together in ever-changing ways for untold generations.

Being creative makes us human. It separates us from the animal kingdom. Today, we get joy from the beauty we see in a painting or hear in a piece of music. They help us to relax by bringing down our stress levels. We live in a digitally connected world where, in an instant, I can learn new things from listening to a TED Talk, reading a blog or following someone on Twitter. I can instantaneously share this new information with whomever I like, and they can pass it onward with the push of a button.

All of this provides opportunities that make us more creative. Through our creativity, we can 'teach' our family, friends, peers and the next generation by sharing our experiences, knowledge and wisdom. Even though we probably don't recognize it, everyone is a teacher because everyone is creative. Every day, no matter who you are, where you reside or what you do, you inevitably teach someone something new, and you will be taught something new yourself.

I cannot emphasize enough the importance of creativity at the centre of our nature. Embrace and celebrate that fact. If, by your upbringing or education, you've been led to believe that you aren't creative, then that wrong can now be put right. You are an awesome creative machine, and once you've accepted that, you will be on the road to unlocking your imagination and creating fantastic new things.

We can now explore how we have used creativity to not only survive, but how we thrived through innovation. This is where we rebel against entrenched ideas, adopt new perspectives, and open the door to exciting new thought and expression.

FROM CREATIVITY TO INNOVATION
IN OUR SOUL

What would you say if I asked who invented the printing press?

You'd inevitably say Gutenberg. That is what I was taught at school, and most people would answer the same.

In fact, that's completely wrong. The answer is that nobody really knows who it was. The reason I know this is that I read a fascinating article on the *History* website, which explained the history of the development of the printing press. It stated that the oldest known printed text — *The Diamond Sutra*, a Buddhist book from Dunhuang, China — dates to around 868 AD, some 530 years before Gutenberg was born. The book was created with a method known as block printing, which utilized panels of hand-carved wood blocks with the text incised in reverse.

Moveable type, which replaced rigid printing blocks with individual letters that could be moved around and reused, was developed by Bi Sheng, an artisan and engineer from Hubei, China, who lived from roughly 970–1051 AD. He created type that was carved into clay and baked into hard blocks that were then arranged on an iron frame that was pressed against an iron plate.

In 1297, when the Chinese engineer, agronomist and politician Wang Zhen printed an illustrated treatise on agriculture and farming practices called *Nung Shu*, he devised a process that used moveable wood type, which produced more precise print. He then created a revolving table that helped typesetters organize their work with more efficiency, which led to greater speed in printing.

In Europe, the printing press did not appear until 150 years after Wang Chen's innovation, when in 1440 the German inventor, printer, publisher and goldsmith Johannes Gutenberg replaced wood with metal and small printing blocks with individual letters, creating the European version of moveable type.

Some 600 years later, in 1968, Evelyn Berezin, a pioneering American computer designer, had the idea for a word processor to simplify the work of secretaries. The device, which was the size of a small refrigerator, allowed users to edit, delete, cut and paste text, which could then be printed out on a cable-connected IBM Selectric typewriter, with its rotating metal ball of type. Today, of course, you don't even have to connect to a computer with a cable, thanks to countless apps that allow one-touch wireless printing.

This evolution of printing methodologies brings to mind the words Mark Twain, who wrote in his 1907 autobiography:

> *"There is no such thing as a new idea. It is impossible. We simply take a lot of old ideas and put them into a sort of mental kaleidoscope. We give them a turn and they make new and curious combinations. We keep on turning and making new combinations indefinitely, but they are the same old pieces of coloured glass that have been in use through all the ages."*

The key word there is 'indefinitely,' meaning we have always tried to take ideas and improve upon them, which has sparked our thoughts in different directions. Being creative allows us to innovate, and it is through innovation that new products, methodologies, works of art and business start-ups appear.

Being creative is in our soul — our emotional soul. Humans love the feeling of creating something new, improving it, and continuing to make it better and better. Creativity is in our soul because it allows us to innovate.

The printing press was envisaged about 2,000 years ago, and in the ensuing centuries, through creative thinking that led to innovation, humans have improved upon it. There is a direct through-line to today, where I am typing this chapter on my Apple Mac and wirelessly printing out the pages via my HP Smart Printing App. It is through innovation like this, over thousands of years, that humans have made unbelievable progress in agriculture, science, medicine, the arts, technology and business.

IN OUR SOUL

Just think of the fantastic things humans have invented. They range from electricity, writing, the steam engine, bicycles, cars and antibiotics to the mobile phone, the world wide web, flight, the microscope, mathematics and soap... to name but a few. Each one of them would have gone through an iterative creative process like the one that developed, and constantly improved, the printing press.

THE HISTORY OF INNOCATION CYCLES

Below, we show waves of innovation across 250 years, from the industrial revolution to sustainable technology.

LONG WAVES OF INNOVATION

The theory of innovation cycles was developed by economist Joseph Schumpeter who coined the term "creative destruction" in 1942. Schumpeter examined the role of innovation in relation to long-wave business cycles.

@MIT Economics

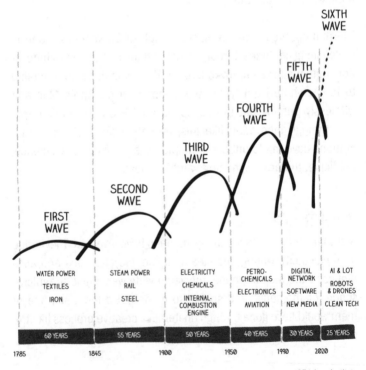

SIXTH WAVE

FIFTH WAVE

FOURTH WAVE

THIRD WAVE

SECOND WAVE

FIRST WAVE

WATER POWER	STEAM POWER	ELECTRICITY	PETRO-CHEMICALS	DIGITAL NETWORK	AI & LOT
TEXTILES	RAIL	CHEMICALS	ELECTRONICS	SOFTWARE	ROBOTS
IRON	STEEL	INTERNAL-COMBUSTION ENGINE	AVIATION	NEW MEDIA	& DRONES / CLEAN TECH

| 60 YEARS | 55 YEARS | 50 YEARS | 40 YEARS | 30 YEARS | 25 YEARS |

1785   1845   1900   1950   1990   2020

@Edelson Institute

KEY BREAKTHROUGHS

FIRST WAVE

DRING THE INDUSTRIAL REVOLUTION, THE FIRST FACTORY EMERGED – A COTTON MILL IN BRITAIN.

THIRD WAVE

HENRY FORD'S MODEL T INTRODUCED THE ASSEMBLY LINE, REVOLUTIONIZING THE AUTOMOTIVE INDUSTRY.

FIFTH WAVE

IN 1990, 2.3M USED THE INTERNET – BY 2016 THIS RREACHED 3.4B.

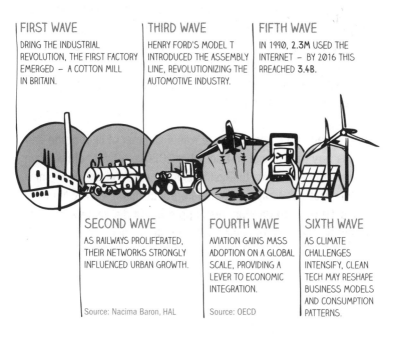

SECOND WAVE

AS RAILWAYS PROLIFERATED, THEIR NETWORKS STRONGLY INFLUENCED URBAN GROWTH.

Source: Nacima Baron, HAL

FOURTH WAVE

AVIATION GAINS MASS ADOPTION ON A GLOBAL SCALE, PROVIDING A LEVER TO ECONOMIC INTEGRATION.

Source: OECD

SIXTH WAVE

AS CLIMATE CHALLENGES INTENSIFY, CLEAN TECH MAY RESHAPE BUSINESS MODELS AND CONSUMPTION PATTERNS.

Being creative is in our soul. It's in our nature to solve the most challenging problems and pursue the most daunting opportunities. From the discovery of penicillin to putting a man on the moon, we have achieved some stunning things. The exciting news is that we can only get more creative, and that leads to further innovation.

The last few years have been a terrible time because of COVID-19. As I write this chapter, the World Health Organization reports that more than 6.2 million individuals worldwide have died of the virus. The sorrow, pain and misery of each victim's death has caused their family and friends has been truly horrific. And all evidence seems to indicate the pandemic will continue to wreak havoc over the coming months and years.

Through all of the despair, there was a glimmer of light at the end of this very dark tunnel. In December 2020, a 90-year-old woman, Margaret Keenan, was the first person on earth to receive the new COVID vaccine. What is remarkable about this is that it normally takes 10 years to develop, test, approve and distribute a vaccine, at an average cost of some £500 million or more. There are normally four stages:

1. Research / drug discovery (2–5 years)
2. Pre-clinical trials (2 years)
3. Clinical development
   Phase 1: Is it safe? (1–2 years)
   Phase 2: Does it activate an immune response? (2–3 years)
   Phase 3: Does it protect against the disease? (2–4 years)
4. Regulatory review and approval (1–2 years)

The vaccine that Margaret received went through this entire process in a single year. So, how did the scientists who worked on creating a safe and effective coronavirus vaccine pull it together so quickly?

That success is in large part attributable to new vaccine technologies being used for the first time. Immunologists were being innovative by doing things in a slightly different way, which proved to be faster and safer than the traditional method of creating a vaccine. And mobilization against a new pandemic should be even quicker next time because scientists have subsequently developed even more innovative ways to create and roll out new vaccines... and the innovation will continue.

Through creative thinking coupled with innovation, the COVID vaccine and follow-up boosters have saved countless lives. That is the power of creative thinking in action.

So, here is the million-dollar question: if we can solve massive problems like this, why don't we put creativity at the centre of everything we do in life? By doing that, we can open up our imagination to brilliant things, create groundbreaking technologies and solve vexing business challenges. The potential benefits are endless.

THE CREATIVE GAP

But, here is the nub of the problem: we don't put creativity at the centre of what we do because of us!

If you asked 100 people whether they're creative, how many would say yes? Well, in 2012, the Silicon Valley software firm Adobe surveyed 5,000 people the US, UK, Germany, France and Japan on that question. There findings were published a report titled 'Global creativity gap.'

According to the findings, the vast majority of people around the world know creativity is crucial to economic expansion, the development of society and their personal growth. Yet, only one in four

There's room for everybody on the planet to be creative and conscious if you are your own person. If you're trying to be like somebody else, then there isn't.

Tori Amos

actually feel they're living up to their creative potential. Why the discrepancy? Let's explore the key findings:

1. Creativity is important. The study found that 80% of those surveyed believe creativity is key to economic growth and 64% feel it is valuable to society. And 75% thought that being creative enables them to make a difference in their own lives, while another two thirds believe it helps them make a difference in the lives of others. In a world in which innovation drives the economy, and more people than ever have the opportunity to be creative, this is not surprising. That's good news, but there's a huge gap in terms of creative application.

2. Creativity is not happening anywhere near as often as it could or should. While 80% of respondents felt we all have the potential to be creative, they also stated that they spend only a third of their time being creative, and only 25% felt they were living up to their creative potential.

Now, imagine if we can move that 25% figure up to 50%. Think what we could achieve — things like the fantastic, world-changing innovations we've already discussed in this chapter. More importantly, what to others might seem like small innovations could for you could be life-altering. What is stopping us achieving this 50%? What precisely is behind our glaring creativity gap? It is, what I call, the inhibitors which are blocking your creativity

Let's start with the first one, our education system, by introducing you to three teachers whose simple act highlights — and shows how we can get around — one of the main impediments to creativity.

Creativity is as important as literacy.

Sir Ken Robinson

PART TWO

UNLOCKING
THE INHIBITORS
TO BOOST YOUR
CREATIVITY

SLOWING DOWN THE HUMAN IMAGINATION
INHIBITOR: EDUCATION

In May 2015, three teachers — Mrs Brown, Mrs Quinn and Mrs Brierley, at Buckton Vale Primary School in Greater Manchester, England — sent a letter to all Year 6 pupils. It was delivered a week before the ten-year-olds were due to take their Standard Assessment Tests (SATs), an exam used in the UK to evaluate a child's educational progress.

The teachers' letter told the youngsters how special and unique they were. It highlighted all the natural skills and abilities they had, and everything that made them smart individuals. They were told how their "laughter can brighten the darkest day," and that the examiners did not know just how "kind, trustworthy and thought-ful" the pupils were.

The following is the text of the letter, which has been in published in national and international newspapers and websites, and shared globally across social media platforms:

Dear Year 6 pupils,

Next week you will sit your SATs tests for maths, reading, spelling, grammar and punctuation. We know how hard you have worked, but there is something very important you must know:

The SATs test does not assess all of what makes each of you special and unique. The people who create these tests and score them do not know each of you the way that we do and certainly not in the way your families do.

They do not know that some of you speak two languages or that you love to sing or draw.

They have not seen your natural talent for dancing or playing a musical instrument.

They do not know that your friends can count on you to be there for them; that your laughter can brighten the darkest day or that your face turns red when you feel shy.

They do not know that you participate in sports, wonder about the future, or sometimes help your little brother or sister after school. They do not know that you are kind, trustworthy and thoughtful and that every day you try to be your very best.

The levels you will get from this test will tell you something, but they will not tell you everything. There are many ways of being smart. You are smart! So, while you are preparing for the test and in the midst of it all, remember that there is no way to 'test' all of the amazing and awesome things that make you, YOU!

It ends with a quote by Aristotle: "Educating the mind without educating the heart is no education at all."

I used this story in the first chapter of my 2020 book, *Inspired Thinking*, where I rethink the meaning of inspired thinking for the

21st century. This letter exemplifies the fundamental idea that every child should be valued for who they are, regardless of ability. I found that to be a very powerful and inspiring message.

But now, I also see this message in a slightly different way. I still strongly believe that every child should be valued for who they are. But it also saddens me that these children who have wonderful creative abilities — like speaking multiple languages, singing, drawing, dancing and playing musical instruments — might be prevented from fulfilling their creative potential as they start to get older.

At some point, the children who'd shown so much creative energy were probably convinced that they weren't creative at all. They were told, by the education system which they went through, that creativity is not really important.

Going back to the Global Creativity Gap study, 80% of respondents said yes when asked if they felt they had the potential to be creative. However, it also found that only 25% felt they were living up to their creative potential. What causes this?

I believe that happens when youngsters leave primary education and move on to secondary education.

UNBLOCK   DO SCHOOLS KILL CREATIVITY?

The most popular TED Talk ever was presented by Sir Kenneth Robinson, an international advisor on education, in 2006. 'Do schools kill creativity?' has been viewed well over 68 million times. It is a brilliant, entertaining and moving case for creating an education system that nurtures, rather than undermines, creativity. In the talk, Sir Kenneth challenges the way we're educating our children.

He champions a radical rethink of our school systems in order to cultivate creativity and acknowledge multiple types of intelligence. He argues that "we don't grow into creativity; we grow out of it. Or rather, we get educated out of it." Yet, he says, "creativity is as important as literacy and we should afford it the same status."

He also points out that if you look at any education system in the world, they all have the same hierarchy of subjects. Starting at the top we have mathematics, science and languages. Then below these are humanities and at the bottom are the arts. But there is also an hierarchy in the arts. In the main, visual arts and music are more valued than drama and dance.

As evidence of how schools kill creativity, he cites the example of a young English girl named Gillian Lynne. At the age of eight, Gillian was viewed as a 'problem student' with a probable learning disorder due to her inability to sit still and concentrate. When her mother sought a medical explanation for the child's constant fidgeting and lack of focus, the doctor suggested they speak privately. As the two adults got up to leave, the doctor turned on the radio. Left alone in a music-filled room, young Gillian began to dance. Observing her through the window, the doctor turned to her mother. "Gillian's not sick," he said. "She's a dancer."

Gillian, who died in 2008, at the age of 92, went on to a long career in ballet, dance and musical theatre, which saw her become one of the world's most successful choreographers. Among her many achievements, she was associated with hits like Sir Andrew Lloyd-Webber's *Cats* and *Phantom of the Opera*. Yet, her school had all but written her off, failing to see her extraordinary talent and focussing on what they thought was a behavioural problem or cognitive impairment.

What can we do about this, as it has affected my own education journey, probably yours and, I'd wager, the majority of people who've been fortunate enough to have been given an education?

DON'T BLAME THE TEACHERS

Teachers are arguably the most important members of our society. They give children a sense of purpose, set them up for success as citizens of the world, and inspire in them the drive to succeed in life. The students of today are the leaders of tomorrow, and teachers are central to preparing them for their future.

Teachers can fulfil many roles. They can provide a support system, for example if home life is complicated. They serve as role models, inspiring students to dream. Teachers can shape opinions and help young people form ideas about society, life and personal goals. They can also expand students' limits and catalyse their creativity.

In his commencement speech to the graduates at University of Western Australia, the comedian, songwriter and musician Tim Minchin said this in his '9 life lessons' talk:

"Please be a teacher. Teachers are the most admirable and important people in the world."

So, no, we must never blame the teachers.

As Sir Kenneth so eloquently summarized, the problems lie with the educational system itself, which — along with society in general — values mathematics, science, languages, history and economics far more than creative endeavours.

"

Every child is an artist, the problem is staying an artist when you grow up.

"

Pablo Picasso

Here's a thought: if we championed the teaching of creativity as much as traditional academic subjects, we could meld imagination, self-expression and divergent thinking with knowledge, logic and the application of scientific and economic principles, leading to innovative new solutions to longstanding problems.

However, the sad reality is that no government would be willing to radically change their education system any time soon. So, what can be done?

BOOST ACCEPT YOU WEREN'T TAUGHT HOW TO BE CREATIVE

You need to understand how your own education probably failed to teach you how to be creative, accept that fact, and try and think slightly differently about it all. Here are three fundamental things you picked up in school that you may need to change if you want to become more creative:

1. THERE MIGHT NOT BE AN ANSWER

A cornerstone of modern education is the exam. The way exams are constructed, you're asked a series of questions designed to demonstrate that you have mastered the material the examiner presented. In school, you spend most of your time repeating back answers to questions that the examiner already knows. It is also true that many modern exams require the mastering of technique and are very formulaic.

In addition, most tests are designed so that there is one best answer that the examiner is looking for in order for you to get full credit. Not only that, most exams are long and have to be completed in a short period of time. That means you are rewarded for finding the best answer, giving it and then moving promptly on to the next question.

Creativity doesn't work like that at all.

THE CREATIVE PROCESS

START ——————————————— END

First, creativity requires answering questions that nobody knows the answer to yet. So, you need to get out of the mindset of figuring out what someone else wants to hear and get into a mode of finding ways to solve a problem.

Second, there are likely to be many different potential solutions to problems that require innovation. To find them, you need to be willing to generate and consider various alternatives, rather than finding one quickly and moving on.

2. SEE MISTAKES AS GOOD THINGS

Success in school is measured by grades. The way you get good grades is to make as few mistakes as possible. So, without realizing it, you have probably internalized a belief that mistakes are bad and that they are to be avoided at all costs.

That strategy makes sense when you are working in an area where the solutions are known, and are just trying to execute those solutions flawlessly. Again, creativity does not work like this. If you're trying to be innovative, there will always be times when conventional ideas and known solutions don't work.

Some people shy away from situations that require creativity because they fear making a mistake. You need to overcome that tendency if you want to be more creative. You need to recognize that creativity and innovation involve lots of mistake making. Many of your initial ideas will be flawed. And, even if you try hard, an innovative approach may fail. Successful innovators learn from their mistakes. You must embrace your errors and learn from them rather than avoiding them.

3. BE PATIENT

The best academic students are often the most conscientious ones. They plan, with a strict timetable, to get their work done on schedule, sequentially ticking off their tasks in a linear way.

Creativity does not have the same linear flow as classwork. In creative pursuits, there may be long periods of time in which you are reading, contemplating, sketching out ideas and test-driving possible solutions. All the while, you may feel like you aren't making any clear progress towards your goal. Only when you hit on a really great idea do you suddenly have the sense that a solution may be in sight.

To be successful in creative endeavours, you have to be willing to tolerate periods in which it feels like you are not making any progress. That can be discouraging, and it's tempting to go back and focus on tasks you can tick off your to-do list. Resist that urge. Keep working, even when it feels like you are moving in circles.

As we've said, creativity is in our DNA, nature and soul. But, to a large extent, our education system does not recognize or nourish this. Hopefully, these three simple ideas — there might not be an answer; see mistakes as good things; be patient — can help you throw off the shackles of your education and unlock your creativity.

PROGRAMMED NOT TO BE CREATIVE
INHIBITOR: WORK

Over the last 25 years I have been involved with seven software and digital services companies as either a chairman, CEO or non-executive director. Along the way I have witnessed three events that threatened those companies, along with millions of others.

The first was in 2000, when a computer flaw known as the Millennium Bug led to the Y2K (Year 2000) scare. In the late 1990s, many experts believed there would be serious computing problems — conceivably bringing down worldwide infrastructures in industries ranging from banking to air travel — when dealing with dates beyond December 31, 1999.

When complicated programs were being written from the 1960s–1980s, computer engineers used a two-digit code for the year. The '19' was left out. Instead of a date reading 1970, it read 70. As the year 2000 approached, programmers realized that computers might not interpret 00 as 2000, but as 1900. This was a potentially catastrophic problem.

For example, power plants depend on routine computer maintenance for safety checks, such as water pressure or radiation levels. Not having the correct date would throw off these calculations and possibly put the populace at risk. Transportation systems also depend on the correct time and date. Airlines in particular were considered at risk, as computers with records of all scheduled flights would be threatened. More pressingly, so were critical on-board software systems in some older planes.

In the end, there were fortunately very few problems. Yet, millions of companies pumped incalculable time, effort and money into contingency planning for potential computer issues as the calendar rolled over to the new millennium.

The second event, which turned out to be very serious indeed, was the financial crash in 2008. The crisis, when a housing market bubble fuelled by reckless lending led to mass loan defaults, was the greatest jolt to the global financial system since the Great Depression of the 1930s. The losses led many financial institutions to fail, pushing the world's banking system to the edge of collapse.

At the time, I was the director of a software company that banked with Royal Bank of Scotland (RBS). In the early- to mid-2000s, RBS had grown from a small, conservative Scottish clearing bank into the largest bank in the world. Large-scale assumption of bad loans escalated as the bank made an unwise £71 billion acquisition based on faulty due diligence. Things came to a head and the house of cards teetered precariously.

On the morning of 8 October 2008, RBS was about to collapse. To prevent this from happening, the UK government stepped in with a £45.5 billion taxpayer-funded bailout. If this had not happened, my company and thousands of others would have faced the very real problem of having no bank facilities and unavailable funds.

Fortunately, with the government's intervention, that did not happen.

The third, and by far most serious, existential threat to enterprises has been the coronavirus. Millions of businesses have been significantly affected by the pandemics, which persists as I write this. Unfortunately, many companies have not survived, others have had to furlough staff, a significant number are now making employees work from home, and most all have been forced to find new ways to do business and change the way they operate.

What links these three big events together?

As described, all posed very serious threats to businesses of every shape and size. From what I've witnessed over the last quarter-century, times when a business is threated are when leadership and staff look for innovative solutions. Times of crisis are when they start wearing their 'creative hats.'

COVID has forced companies to come up with creatively innovative ways of trying to survive, work differently and smarter, and keep their customers and attract new ones. Becoming creative under fire has made many of these companies more resilient and determined, as we also saw them do to prepare for the Millennium Bug and survive the Great Recession of 2008–09.

But I have also observed that when the immediate threat has been managed or eliminated, businesses revert back to being less creative and innovative. And the question is, why?

First, some context. As noted, the crash of 2008 forced leaders to get creative in order to weather the crisis.

Two years later, IBM published the results of a global survey of more than 1,500 CEOs, titled 'Capitalizing on complexity.' A majority of respondents said they found creativity to be the single most important leadership trait for success at that point in time.

That was followed in 2016 by a report from the global consultancy PricewaterhouseCoopers (PwC), titled 'The talent challenge: harnessing the power of human skills in the machine age.' PwC interviewed 4,446 chief executives in 89 countries and territories, and found that the top priority for their organizations at the time was innovation. Yet, 77% of these leaders reported struggling to find the creativity and innovation skills they needed.

How do we square this circle? If, as we've said, we are born with creativity in our DNA, and business leaders say mobilizing creativity and innovation is their top priority, how is it that they can't seem to find the talent necessary to drive their business forward?

As noted, when there's no longer a significant threat, most conventional leaders go back to 'the norm' in terms of how they operate. Taking risks, a key ingredient in creativity, is no longer encouraged, and the innovative impulse gets tamped down.

For the most part, this isn't because leaders are somehow opposed to creativity. On the contrary, as the IBM and PwC reports showed, most believe in the value of innovative new ideas. At senior and middle management levels, though, creativity is unintentionally undermined every day in work environments that were established to maximize profit, reduce costs and facilitate coordination, teamwork, productivity and control.

The journalist Pilita Clark, a business columnist at *The Financial Times*, wrote a fascinating 2019 article headlined, 'How the modern office is killing our creativity.' She highlighted an event where ad agency founder Roger Mavity and design guru Stephen Bayler talked about their recently published book, *How to Steal Fire*, which looked at creativity in the business world. One of their main arguments was that creativity was being inhibited by the design of the modern office. They asserted that big, open-plan workspaces – which proponents say encourage collaboration and productivity – actually kill creativity because a key creative catalyst is solitude. The creative process, they say, is an individual activity rather than a collective undertaking.

The authors said that while most leaders believe that teamwork, brainstorming and 'away days' help their employees become more creative and innovative, this is one of the "great myths" of modern business. In a group dynamic, they argued, when people try to figure out a problem, they tend to either show off to impress or politely back each other's thoughts, no matter how poor they are. Either way, because responsibility is shared, the pressure to come up with solutions is reduced.

This phenomenon even has a name, the Ringelmann Effect, after French engineer Max Ringelmann, who in 1913 observed that individual productivity – and, logically, creativity – falls as group size increases. It is also called Social Loafing.

SOCIAL LOAFING

100% EFFORT   93% EFFORT EACH   85% EFFORT EACH

SOCIAL LOAFING IS THE PHENOMENON WHERE PEOPLE TEND TO EXERT LESS
EFFORT TO ACHIEVE A GOAL WHEN THEY WORK IN A GROUP THAN WHEN
WORKING ALONE. THIS IS MOSTLY APPLICABLE WHEN INDIVIDUAL CONRTIBUTIONS
ARE NOT OBVIOUS.

@deepuasok

Being around others can be helpful when you're trying to gather
background information or understand the dimensions of a problem, but not when it comes to doing really complex, innovative work.
Brainstorming and teamwork are mainstays of modern business
life, driving endless meetings and other bureaucratic distractions
that conspire to interrupt focused thought, creative or otherwise.
These practices persist, despite their obvious drawbacks.

"

The brain is a wonderful organ. It starts the moment you get up and doesn't stop until you get into the office.

"

Robert Frost

The same law of diminishing returns applies if you are a school-teacher, supermarket cashier, nurse or construction worker. You will have little time for solitude, and you'll be constantly restrained by the work practices you have to follow, none of which will aid your ability to use your creative mind.

If that is the environment your work in, this will greatly inhibit your ability to be creative, regardless of your industry sector, job title or pay grade.

BOOST   UNLEASHING YOUR CREATIVITY, EVEN AT WORK

To be clear, I am not promising to help you become wildly creative in your work, although this may well be one of the outcomes of reading this book. My aim is to give you some ideas that can help you become more creative and innovative, both at work and in your private life. In the end, I am trying to bridge the creative void that the hustle and grind of the traditional workaday world has instilled in you.

To do this, I want to focus on a short list of triggers that will help you unleash your creativity.

TRIGGER 1   RIGHT LOCATION

Whatever your occupation, you need to find the right physical setting to spark that creative fire.

Over the years, I have attended many meeting, conferences and seminars. Some have been in Edinburgh, where all my offices have been based, while others have elsewhere in the UK, as well as in various European and American cities.

Wherever I find myself, I try once or twice a week to take the time to visit somewhere new and interesting, which I know will help calm my brain and give me the solitude to think. When I am in Edinburgh, I will pop into the Waterstones bookshop on Princes Street. As soon as I walk through the door, I know I have entered a place of inspiration, where the shelves are packed with ideas, wisdom and knowledge. If I have to travel to another city, I allow some time to check out somewhere new and different, and always get the same calm, reflective feeling.

Looking back, I'm convinced my creativity has increased when I've found myself in these new locations. I think this is because the stimuli of unfamiliar surroundings and experiences unleash that creativity. Key to this is the fact that I am usually on my own, and as we've said, solitude and creativity go hand in hand.

And I can assure you that you needn't to go to London, Paris or Chicago to experience a new and inspiring setting. My guess is that there will be villages, towns and attractions close to where your work that you've have never visited. Or there will be different bookstores, museums, art galleries and parks you could visit.

So, during your lunchtime, or at the end of your working day, try to pop out to some such places from time to time, as the change of scenery will be sure to ignite your creative mind.

TRIGGER 2 RIGHT ENVIRONMENT

Another great way to trigger your creativity is to work somewhere different on a regular basis.

While Trigger 1 involves clearing your mind with an unstructured walk through a different setting, this one calls for actually setting up camp in a different setting for the workday. The nature of much modern work, and today's information technology, give a great many of us the opportunity to be *digital nomads*. We're simply not as 'chained to the mast' as we used to be. I don't mean that you should be constantly swapping out workspaces, but it's worth trying for at least a few hours a week. Whatever you do for a living, if you want to become more creative in your thinking, a great trigger is to find a new space to work in.

What you are trying to do is to find a place to go about your work that differs from your drab, boring old surroundings. This will give you space and time for solitude and calmness, which will allow your brain to wander and experience new thoughts and insights. New surroundings are a proven catalyst for divergent thinking.

TRIGGER 3 RIGHT PEOPLE

Just meeting people can be also the trigger for creativity. But how do you find time to meet up with others when you're working?

Try turning to the internet, where you can 'meet' a whole world of new people, with interesting things to say, on Wikipedia, YouTube, blogs, Instagram, TED Talks, LinkedIn, podcasts and Twitter. Among all the pros and cons of the digital realm, it's certainly chock-full of fascinating, inspiring people, sharing wildly diverse experiences, views, perspectives and ideas.

Or maybe join an online book club, download a seminar or presentation on a topic you know little about, enrol in an online course on a subject you're really interested in, or watch a Netflix or Amazon documentary on an area that's entirely new to you. With the power of digital technology at your fingertips, you can find, see and listen to virtually anyone, anytime, anywhere around the globe.

If you spend at least 45 minutes, two to three times a week, in a different setting, or meeting new and inspiring people, you'll be amazed how much more creative and innovative your life can become.

Decide here and now that you won't let your occupation, comfy surroundings and predictable old routines kill your creative potential. Get out there and mix it up a bit!

THE DANGER OF
THE NEWS
INHIBITOR: NEWS

I recently bought a book, *Stop Reading the News: A Manifesto for a Happier, Calmer and Wiser Life*, by one of my favourite authors, Rolf Dobelli. I was aware that Dobelli had been planning to write a book about avoiding the news because he'd written an essay about it in 2013, which was published on his website.

The essay, titled 'News lunch,' expounded the theory that reading, listening to or watching too much news is as bad as eating too much sugar. "Today, we have reached the same point in relation to information overload that we faced 30 years ago with food intake," he wrote. "We are beginning to recognize how toxic news can be."

In his book, Dobelli lists many reasons why you should dial-back your news intake. Chapter titles include: 'News is a waste of time'; 'News is irrelevant'; 'News makes us passive'; 'News is toxic to your body.' In fact, 19 of the chapters start with 'News...' to drive home his point.

I have to say that I agree with some of his arguments, but not necessarily all of them. These days, news is literally everywhere. We have 24-hour news channels, print and digital newspapers, accusations of 'fake news' and social media platforms that allow anyone in the world to post anything they want without a reality check.

One of Dobelli's observations that I totally agree with is that news kills creativity. However, I see it a bit differently than he does. He claims that one reason exceptionally talented people often produce their most creative works at a young age is that their brains enjoy a wide, uninhabited space that emboldens them to come up with and pursue new ideas.

Dobelli states that he does not know of a single truly creative mind who is a news junkie — not a writer, composer, mathematician, physician, scientist, musician, designer, architect or painter. On the other hand, he says, he does know a bunch of uncreative minds who consume news like drugs. "If you want to come up with old solutions, read news," he says. "If you are looking for new solutions, don't."

I have to disagree with him on this point. A lot of the material for my books comes from the news. Of the five books I've written, a number of chapters have been inspired by articles I've read in *The Times* and the *Guardian* newspapers, heard on news radio stations, and seen on news websites and blog posts. These articles are the sparks that ignite my creative thinking and ultimately feature in my books.

However, where I do see news killing creativity is that consuming lots of it causes us to be more stressed and anxious. And this, undeniably, is an inhibitor to creativity.

A fascinating article was published by *Time* magazine in 2018, titled 'You asked: Is it bad for you to read the news constantly?' It looked at a study by the American Psychological Association indicating that, for many Americans, "news consumption has a downside." It showed one in ten US adults checks the news every hour, and 20% of Americans "constantly" monitor their social media feeds, immersing them in a never-ending deluge of headlines. The study reported that "more than half of Americans say the news causes them stress, and many report feeling anxiety, fatigue or sleep loss as a result."

Most people would agree that it is important to stay informed on the major issues of the day. And, in these crazy times, it's not surprising that some of this could be stressful. But being inundated with so many news sources, with so much *doom and gloom* coverage, so much of the time — until it seems that we're drinking from an infernal fire hose — can't be very good for us.

"

The people will believe what the media tells them they believe.

"

George Orwell

Graham Davey, a Professor Emeritus of Psychology at Sussex University and editor of *The Journal of Experimental Psychopathology*, has done research showing that negative TV news is a significant mood-changer, and the moods it tends to produce are sadness and anxiety. "Our studies also showed that this change in mood exacerbates the viewer's own personal worries, even when those worries are not directly relevant to the news stories being broadcast," he says.

He also points out that "the way that news is presented and the way that we access news has changed significantly over the last 15 to 20 years" and these changes "have often been detrimental to general mental health."

Davey says today's news is "increasingly visual and shocking," and points to the inclusion of smartphone videos and audio clips as examples. These bystander-captured images can be so intense that they can cause symptoms of acute stress, he says, like problems sleeping, mood swings, aggressive behaviour or even full-blown PTSD.

Beyond the impact on mental well-being, there is growing evidence that overdosing on news can harm your physical health. Stress-related hormones, like cortisol and adrenalin, have been linked to inflammation associated with rheumatoid arthritis, cardiovascular disease and other serious health concerns.

So, if the evidence suggests the news can stress people out, why do they keep going back for more? For one thing, it's entertaining, Davey says. The human brain is also wired to pay attention to information that scares or unsettles us — a concept known as 'negativity bias.'

Loretta Breuning, a former Professor of Management at California State University and author of *Habits of a Happy Brain*, explains the concept of negativity bias. "In a state of nature," she says, "our survival depends on finding rewards and avoiding harm, but avoiding harm takes priority." So, the human brain is attracted to troubling information because it's programmed to detect threats, not to overlook them.

"This can make it hard for us to ignore the negatives and seek out the positives around us," she says. "Our brain is predisposed to go negative, and the news we consume reflects this."

If, as the evidence suggests, watching, listening to or reading the news is bad for your mental health, and consequently inhibits your creativity, what can you do about it?

BOOST   GO ON A NEWS DIET

Davey, the psychology journal editor, advises the following: "Try to be aware of how [the news] changes your mood or makes your thoughts more negative." If you seem more anxious when you consuming loads of daily news, take a break. Put on some mood-lifting music, exercise or tune into something on TV that makes you laugh. All of these can help reduce anxiety levels.

Bottom line: the remedy to uncomfortable *news bloat* may be going on a news diet.

You could also pare back on your habit by removing most of your news apps and committing to limit consumption to a certain time of the day. For example, you might scroll through *BBC News* or the

New York Times website when you're having breakfast. And then, after work, turn on a local TV news programme for a half-hour. Try to not watch or read the news before you go to bed, as this could wind you up and make it more difficult to fall asleep.

Staying informed is a good thing but when it comes to your creativity, incessant information overload can spell trouble.

"News is not an infectious and contagious pathogen like anthrax or the Ebola virus that impacts humans in relatively predicable ways," says Chris Peters, an Associate Professor of Media and Communication at Aalborg University Copenhagen. "It's extremely complicated – if not impossible – to predict how people in the aggregate will respond to news."

Peters says we shouldn't focus on the amount of news we consume each day, but rather on the ways we engage with it in relation to our everyday lives and the people we interact with. If you find that your news habit is messing with your relationships or general well-being, it may be helpful to make some changes.

Stress is a known creativity killer, and the news of the day can certainly be stressful, and going on a news diet is a great way of clearing some space for creative thinking.

In summary, try to take these six simples steps:

1. Avoid all news coverage completely for a couple of days.
2. When easing back in, limit the time you read, watch or listen to the news to twice a day.
3. If you have a number of news feeds on your phone or tablet, pare them down to two – max.
4. Reduce the time spent reading newspapers, perhaps deciding that you'll read the paper on some days and not others.
5. If you discuss the news with others, keep it short and cursory, and try not to get into heated debates.
6. Try to stay somewhat detached when consuming or discussing the news.

At the start of your news diet, it might be tough to tighten the belt, as there are so many things happening. It's natural to be curious about the world around you, and you're frankly hooked on the buzz. However, abstaining from the news entirely for a few days, and then reengaging to a limited extent, will make you feel more peaceful and less stressed, and you'll be on the road to developing a much healthier habit.

A news diet will teach you to be mentally free and able to shape your own points of view. It will filter out an overabundance of unimportant details, mute the cacophony of battling opinions, and help you feel happier and more at peace.

And this, as you gradually clear the decks, will increase your ability to be freethinking and creative.

THE BIRD'S NEST
INHIBITOR: CONCRETE

I live about 25 miles outside of Edinburgh, Scotland's capital and the country's second-most populous city. After the easing of the first COVID lockdown, it was quite strange making my first trip into the city since the pandemic had started. The place was completely empty of people and cars. On once-busy thoroughfares like George Street or Queen Street, where it would have taken 20 minutes to travel 400 metres, I seemed to have the place to myself.

But what struck me the most was the proliferation of new buildings since I'd last driven those streets. In the centre of Edinburgh, a huge development of offices, shops and a five-star hotel was more than half completed. In other parts of the city, large apartment complexes were being finished. And, seemingly everywhere, new hotels were being built. As I drove back home, I also saw that the city's boundaries were visibly expanding outward, as more and more new housing developments were being constructed.

A few weeks later, I read a fascinating article on the *BBC News* website from environmental reporter Mark Kinver. Headlined 'Millions "lack access" to parks and green places,' it referenced a study that had just been published by the charity Fields in Trust. It cited a growing body of research linking access to natural, outdoor space to better health and well-being, while noting that more than 2.5 million people in the UK no longer lived within a 10 minute walking distance of a park or a green space.

Another study, carried out by a team from the European Centre for Environment and Human Health at the University of Exeter, reported that living in an urban area with green spaces has a long-lasting, positive impact on peoples' mental well-being.

This all brought me back to drive into Edinburgh, where I saw all that new concrete, glass and steel development. The city was growing at an amazing rate. I know we need to build affordable housing, beautiful hotels and new shops to lure back visitors, and additional office space to attract new companies. However, we also need to take heed of these studies. Overdevelopment, without counterbalancing grassy, tree-lined expanses, will have an adverse impact of everyone involved.

And we could be talking about any city in the world. The more concrete we pour, expanding our urban centres outward, the more important it becomes to save, and create, the green spaces that are so crucial.

And, of course, once again there is a tie-in between overall health and well-being and the ability to tap into the creative spirit within.

UNBLOCK   FOREST BATHING

It is well documented that any physical activity can reduce stress and anxiety. But there's something equally special about just being in nature, whether in an urban park, a suburban green space, or on a getaway to a beach or the woods. Stretch out on a sunny hillside, watch the clouds drift by and let the chorus of birdsong wash over you. Feel the stress melt away, the feel-good hormones surge, and you'll automatically immerse into that creative space.

Let me give you a great example of someone who has looked into this for many years: Dr Qing Li of the Nippon Medical School in Tokyo. Every day Dr Qing heads to a leafy park close to his office. It is not that he wants to eat his lunch there; he believes the time spent under the trees' canopy is a critical factor in the fight against diseases of the mind and body.

Then, once a month, Li spends three days in forests near Tokyo, using all five senses to connect with the environment and clear his mind. He believes this practice of *shinrin-yoku* — literally, 'forest bathing' — has the power to counter illnesses, including, depression and anxiety. He maintains that it also boosts the immune system, lowers blood pressure and aids sleep.

Li is one of the world's experts on this practice, which emerged in Japan in the 1980s. He was part of the team that carried out an experiment in 2014 where participants were assigned to walk either in a forest or an urban centre — taking walks of equal length and difficulty — while having their heart rate, blood pressure and other physiological factors measured.

Results showed that those who walked in forests had significantly lower heart rates and higher heart rate variability, which indicated there were more relaxed and less stressed than those who walked in urban settings. The researchers concluded that there's something about being in nature that had a beneficial effect on stress reduction, above and beyond what physical exercise alone might have produced.

> **It is the marriage of the soul with nature that makes the intellect fruitful, and gives birth to imagination.**

Henry David Thoreau

Another study, carried out by the Finnish Forest Research Institute, also found that city dwellers who paid short-term visits to urban nature areas, like public gardens or parks, experienced stress relief. Those who strolled for as little as 20 minutes through an urban park or woodland reported significantly lower stress than those who walked through a bustling city centre.

These studies and others provide evidence that being in natural spaces – or just looking out a window onto a natural scene, or even watching a nature documentary – is good for us. And yes, as you knew I would say, this inevitably has a positive effect on our creative capacity. The more creative you become, the less stressed and anxious you will be, which increases your well-being and happiness. And this cycle repeats itself, time and time again.

I'll talk more about the importance of spending time in nature later in this book, under the header 'More stuff, less creativity.' The idea there is to reduce your time spent thinking about material goods.

BOOST   THE INCREDIBLE NATURAL WORLD

I am very fortunate that my home office is situated at the end of our garden. The office overlooks large trees, bushes and plants, and I can sit and watch nature at play, through the four seasons, from my desk.

Some of the frequent visitors to my garden are wood pigeons, which are truly amazing birds. They mate for life and live as a couple. They return to same nesting site each year, rebuilding and making repairs to their nests.

What I find astounding is the structural strength and beauty of these classic, round-shaped bird's nests. Regardless the weather conditions, from torrential rain to 30–40 mph winds, the nest holds, protecting the pigeons and their young.

And this is a fundamental characteristic of all nesting bird habitats around the globe. Not only do these amazing habitats protect the birds' young, generation after generation, but they also inspire humans to create fantastic structures of our own. Nature has become the spark that fires up man's imagination.

For example, the design of nests inspired the architecture firm Herzog and de Menron to design and build the remarkable Bird's Nest Stadium for the 2008 Beijing Olympics. The façade consists of thousands of steel 'twigs', infilled with translucent panels. This provided the same insulating qualities as feathers, mud and moss in a real bird's nest.

Nike shoe designers studied mountain goats to develop an all-terrain trainer, the Goatek Traction. Japan's Shinkansen bullet train is modelled on the kingfisher's aerodynamic beak. Swiss engineer George de Mestral observed the tiny hooks on burrs that had latched on to the fabric loops in his woven pants during a hunting trip, leading him to develop Velcro.

The list of innovations that have been inspired by nature is significant. The more you study it and spend more time in it, your well-being and happiness will increase, leading you to become more creative. Animal, insects, marine life and plants are the most skilled creators and inventors, and just 'being in and observing it' will be so beneficial for you.

Just observe, and see what it teaches you. The natural world is the ultimate library, accessible to everyone and ready to reveal its wonders. It is also the best teacher. Study, experience and embrace it. It will fire up your creativity like nothing else will, and you'll see your stress and anxiety levels drop precipitously.

REBELS AND MISFITS
INHIBITOR: STEREOTYPES

If you were asked to name the most famous TV advert ever, which would you pick?

Some might suggest 1973's nostalgically cinematic 'Boy on the bike' spot for the UK's Hovis bakeries. Others would point to Coca Cola's uplifting 1971 'I'd like to buy the world a Coke' commercial. What about the 'Honda Cog' ad from 2003, with its Rube Goldberg jumble of cascading car parts, or how about Levi's commercial from 1985 'Laundrette 501.'

All are memorable, as are so many others, but for me it would have to be Apple's 1997 stunner, 'Here's to the crazy ones.'

Narrated by actor Richard Dreyfuss, the commercial salutes more than a dozen 20th century cultural icons. Over black-and-white images of figures like Jimi Hendrix, Bob Dylan, Maria Callas, John Lennon, Joan Baez and Dr Martin Luther King, Jr, Dreyfus extols the power of bold ideas.

''Here's to the crazy ones, the misfits, the rebels, the troublemakers, the round pegs in the square holes... the ones who see things differently — they're not fond of rules... You can quote them, disagree with them, glorify or vilify them, but the only thing you can't do is ignore them because they change things... they push the human race forward, and while some may see them as the crazy ones, we see genius, because the ones who are crazy enough to think that they can change the world, are the ones who do."

I think that copy is brilliantly moving and inspiring because it taps into the creative streak in all of us.

Yet, as fundamentally *human* as creativity is, many people think they're incapable of expressing it. They don't think they can do so because, in their minds, 'creatives' think, feel and behave differently from the vast majority of people.

They see overtly creative people as the rebels, the crazy ones.

My guess is that, for most people, the image of 'creative change-maker' that Apple tried to convey is simply not them. One reason for this, as highlighted in Chapters 4 and 5, is that the education system and the work environment that shaped us were calibrated to produce the opposite of rebels, misfits or troublemakers. From an early age, we are taught to follow the rules, and over the years the pressure to 'fit in' only increases.

You may have gone to school with rebellious types, who challenged authority, pushed boundaries and were likely the ones most teachers found difficult to manage. In the workplace, most managers will see unorthodox mavericks as being difficult to lead and a poor fit with conformist team dynamics.

The pressure to fit in, and the stereotyping of those who don't, is one of the great inhibitors to creativity. Creative types are often seen as oddly anti-establishment and unorthodox. Some even consider creativity "the realm of the tortured soul." Think of Sylvia Plath,

Kurt Cobain or Vincent Van Gogh, all of whom struggled with mental health issues. Think of the hard drinking, drug-fuelled rock stars, who are adored by their fans for their creative output, but whose personal lives tend to be quite erratic.

It is no wonder, then, that creative people can seem very alien to many. And, it follows that if you can't relate to them, you're probably convinced that you can't be creative.

UNBLOCK   REDRAW THE BALANCE

A short 2017 video called 'Redrawing the balance,' produced by the charity Inspiring the Future, highlights the longstanding view that some occupations are for men and some are for women. It shows a teacher asking a class of six-year-olds to draw a surgeon, then a firefighter and finally a fighter pilot. When the children have completed the task, the teacher asks, "Who would like to meet a real surgeon, firefighter and a fighter pilot?" The children shoot up their hands, and into the classroom come all three. The surgeon is a woman in her scrubs. The firefighter and fighter pilot, removing their helmets, are revealed to be women as well.

The children are visibly shocked. Then, we see the drawings they'd produced — 61 depicted men, and just five were of women. The video finishes with powerful statement: "It's time to redraw the balance."

It was a striking illustration of the gender stereotypes that still exist in society. From an early age, we are conditioned to regard certain occupations as 'male' or 'female.'

Of course, there is no exclusively men's occupation or women's occupation. Women can pursue, and succeed in, any career they choose. Similarly, there is no right or wrong image of what a creative person should be. We absolutely need to redraw the balance to ensure that children understand that women can do the same as men, whether it is in sport, the arts or any sort of occupation. We also need to redraw the image of a creative person so that more people can be encouraged to be creative.

Still, it's hard to avoid falling into the traps of stereotyping. False beliefs about our abilities easily turn into a voice of self-doubt in our heads, which can be hard to ignore. Trying not to follow the crowd at school, in social settings or in the workplace is difficult. Over the last couple of decades, psychologists have drawn attention to the so-called 'stereotype threat,' a fear of doing something that would confirm negative perceptions among a group that we're members of or want to join.

There's a difference between being yourself and being your stereotype.

Iggy Azalea

If you have a stereotyped view of what creative people are — rebellious, mavericks, anti-establishment and unorthodox — you might worry that if you tried to become more creative, your family, friends, colleagues and superiors would pigeonhole you too. Consequently, your subconscious mind may see creativity as a stereotype threat.

So, what do we do about this? Just accept it and move on? Or, perhaps, we're looking at it from the wrong perspective.

Instead, maybe we should ask if we need a new definition of the word *rebel*, and whether the defining characteristics aren't really all that threatening. In fact, if you started to understand, and learn how to foster, these rebel characteristics— to become *a rebel with a cause* — they might lead you to become more creative.

And, could it be possible that some of these traits and behaviours are already present in your makeup, but you're unaware of them? Could recognizing and celebrating them be a key to tapping your inner creative reservoir?

The likely answer is 'yes,' even among the most staid and unadventurous of us.

And with that, let me introduce you to an award-winning researcher and academic who has identified and examined these rebel characteristics.

BOOST   BECOME A REAL REBEL

The expert in this area is Francesca Gino, a Professor of Business Administration at Harvard Business School who focuses on why people make the decisions they do at work. In her 2019 book, *Rebel Talent: Why it Pays to Break the Rules at Work and in Life*, Gino describes the creative rebel.

She describes rebels as people who are deviants – by definition, those who depart from usual or accepted standards – in various fields, but in a positive and constructive way. They challenge the established norms and do things that make them different from the crowd, while operating within the norm. Her rebels don't necessarily break the law, but they are disruptive, unorthodox and apt to get in trouble.

According to Gino, rebels tend to have actively cultivated five characteristics or talents:

1. **NOVELTY**: A desire to seek out challenge and *the new*. Novelty is a stimulant for creativity. To be novel means to experience something new, original or unusual.
2. **CURIOSITY**: The impulse to always ask 'Why?' Curiosity is a safe, non-threating way of being rebellious in the world.
3. **PERSPECTIVE**: The ability to constantly broaden their view of the world.
4. **DIVERSITY**: A tendency to challenge pre-determined social roles and reach out those who may appear different.
5. **AUTHENTICITY**: Rebels embrace *the authentic* in everything they do, remaining open and vulnerable in order to connect with and learn from others.

Can anyone be a rebel? According to Gino, absolutely. The goal is to make it possible for people to become more comfortable being uncomfortable. Most of us are not born rebels. But Gino found in her research, after trying the rebel life, no one wants to go back! And that's terrific news if you want to become more creative.

In her book, she sums up the eight principles of becoming a "new type of rebel."

1. **SEEK OUT THE NEW**: It is important to break away from routines and find inspiration in unlikely places.
2. **ENCOURAGE CONSTRUCTIVE DISSENT**: We often seek out the opinion most likely to match ours. Rebels fight that instinct, finding ways to encourage conflict and disagreement.
3. **OPEN CONVERSATIONS, DON'T CLOSE THEM**: Rebels are willing to keep an open mind.
4. **REVEAL YOURSELF AND REFLECT**: Rebels focus on their strengths, but are honest about their weaknesses and make an effort to be mindful of both.
5. **LEARN EVERYTHING. THEN FORGET EVERYTHING!** Successful rebels understand the importance of mastering the fundamentals in what they want to achieve, but never become slaves to the rules.
6. **FIND FREEDOM IN CONSTRAINTS**: Many people think they can't innovate because the parameters of their job are too rigid. Rebels work through, and even find inspiration in, constraints.
7. **LEAD FROM THE TRENCHES**: Rebels are willing to get their hands dirty, and their family, friends, peers and bosses respect them for that.
8. **FOSTER HAPPY ACCIDENTS**: Rebels know the value of a mistake or unplanned event that results in a beneficial outcome or pleasant surprise. They realize that a mistake can unlock a breakthrough.

According to Gino, rebelling is slowly becoming the new norm, and it might be wise to adopt a more rebellious approach. Becoming this new type of rebel will be exciting, energizing and will boast your levels of creativity.

So, come on over and join the 'crazy ones!'

BLISS STATIONS
INHIBITOR: TECH

A big event occurred this summer in the Francis household. It became an 'empty nest.' My eldest son left home about eight years ago, and now lives in Edinburgh. My daughter left home five years ago, and lives in Glasgow. And my youngest son left home this summer to go the University of Dundee.

So, it's now just my wife and me, along with our Golden Retrievers, Archie and Harris, living in our house. What's great about this is that even though we miss our children, they are all close enough to be able to pop back home for a weekend or for us to go and visit them. But I have to say that there are some advantages of having an empty nest. When I go to the fridge for a beer, there is still beer left. When I go on a Zoom meeting, the internet speed is good, as nobody's downloading a massive, grid-dimming computer game. I sleep at night knowing that I am not going to be jolted awake at 3:00 am by one of my kids crashing into the house after a night out.

I think, though, that the main benefit is that we're no longer bound by familial terms and conditions for holidays. For instance, if the weather is nice in May or September, I can hop onto Airbnb, decide where we'd like to go and see what's available. If I find a place that's looks great, we book it.

And that is exactly happened this year. In the first part of 2022, I had been incredibly busy with work and felt I needed a break.

My wife and I love the Scottish Highlands, especially the magical ruggedness of the Isle of Skye. So, I found a beautiful house in the capital, Portree, and we booked it for a week.

Now, I've always found it difficult to forget about work and relax. So many holidays seemed to come and go without me really unwinding and settling down. I finally realized, shortly before we left for that trip to Skye, that *digital overload* was a big contributor to the uptight state I'd work myself into.

In stumbling across an iPhone function that tracks my screen time, I was shocked by the number of hours I spent each day on social media apps, news sites, podcasts, webcasts and, in particular, my e-mail accounts, text streams and WhatsApp. The average for the month of April was four hours and 32 minutes per day. Let me say that again: I was literally fiddling with my smartphone for four and a half hours a day! If you multiply by 365 days, I realized I was spending nearly 66 days of the year on my mobile phone. Even as I write this sentence, I am genuinely dumbfounded by that fact.

To be fair, I need my phone for work, including sending e-mails, joining Zoom meetings or doing research for my latest book. But still, 66 days a year!

This got me thinking that whatever I am doing — whether sitting at my desk working, playing golf, at the pub or away on holiday — my phone is always on. It's never more than 12 inches from my hand, and I always have one eye on it, on the lookout for *incoming*. When I hear the ping that signals a new notification, I just have to look at it. This struck me as madness. I was just about to travel to one of the most beautiful places in the world, but I was always going to be 'switched on.'

Technology is a useful servant but a dangerous master.

Christian Lous Lange

At that point I made a life-altering decision. As soon as we'd locked the front door and got into the car to start to drive to Skye, I switched my phone off. I did not turn it back on until we'd finished our holiday. If someone had urgently needed to contact us, I'm sure they would have found a way of contacting my wife, even though she hardly ever uses her mobile phone. I also made the decision to power down my laptop, and keep it off, for the duration.

It turned out that being switched off allowed me to have one of the most relaxing, thoroughly chilled holidays of my life. And, during one of our walks, I also realized that creativity is about connecting — connecting with things that will inspire you — but, paradoxically, you must also disconnect so that you can think, meditate and give you brain a well-earned rest.

And the best way that I have found to do that is to switch off my phone and my laptop.

So, why is switching off so important for creativity? Read on...

UNBLOCK   SWITCH OFF

In *Keep Going* — one in a trilogy of books about creativity in the digital age — bestselling author Austin Kleon talks about how to disconnect from the world in order to connect with yourself. Silence and solitude are crucial, Kleon insists. Our modern world of smart-phones, tablets, laptops, computers, push notifications, e-mails, texts, streaming devices, 24/7 news cycles and constant contact is completely at odds with the notion of harnessing creativity to solve a problem, find new inspiration or continue a creative endeavour.

Kleon cites the book *The Power of Myth*, by Joseph Campbell and Bill Moyers, in which they say that everyone should build a "bliss station." "This is a place where you can simply experience and bring forth what you are and what you might be," they write. "This is the place of creative incubation. At first you may find that nothing happens there. But if you have a sacred place and use it, something eventually will happen."

I love the concept of a bliss station, whether it is a physical place or a certain time of the day. My time for doing this is when I am walking my Golden Retrievers on the beach where I live, with my phone off or in silent mode.

I find that when I combine switching off with a walk on the beach, my ability to think creatively is enhanced tenfold. I might be struggling to start a new chapter for a book I'm writing, or needing inspiration to help solve a problem. Whatever it is, this particular bliss station usually moves me into a more creative mindset.

The key word here is 'usually,' because even when I'm in my bliss station, and walking peacefully along with the dogs, I am still susceptible to the creativity-blocking phenomenon of 'brain chatter.'

BRAIN CHATTER

Brain chatter is the inner dialogue that constantly goes on in your head. The good news is that this is completely normal; it's an inescapable part of life. From the moment you wake up, until the moment you fall asleep, this inner background noise is always there. It may be quiet at times, only to become louder in certain situations.

The problem is that when you need to focus your mind on a certain creative endeavour, the constant flow of irrelevant, useless, distracting thoughts makes creativity a non-starter.

One of the characteristics of brain chatter is the same thoughts repeating, over and over again, in a loop. Some of these thoughts are positive, which can help creativity. Too often, though, these repetitive thoughts are negative, which can intensify stress and anxiety, and hamper your creativity.

It can be difficult to switch off this brain chatter, but you can train your mind to do so. This allows you to control your thoughts, rather than being controlled by them.

I only really understood how to do this very recently, with the help of a good friend. Dave is the person I check in with when I start to feel my anxiety levels rise and negative brain chatter increase. It always happens the same way: something acts as a trigger — perhaps something I read or see on TV — and I get swept into a swirl of negative thoughts. My anxiety and stress levels rise, and any attempt to do anything remotely creative is out of the question.

That's when I call Dave for a chat. For more than 25 years, Dave was a practicing mental health professional. He is retired now, but he's is still there for me, with a wealth of experience helping people with their challenges.

It was Dave who suggested an age-old way to reduce brain chatter when I wanted to be creative. He suggested that I learn how to meditate. There is so much published scientific and medical evidence pointing to mediation as a powerful tool to help switch off your brain. And you don't have to jet off to an Indian ashram to learn how — there are loads of apps and websites that will teach you how to mediate. Many are so-called guided meditations, where a facilitator actually talks you through the entire exercise. All I needed was to find the one that would be most useful for me.

And so it is that I regularly use the popular Calm app, which received Apple's 2017 App of the Year Award. It gives you access to loads of podcasts that can help with mental health well-being. I did the 30-day introduction to meditation, where each podcast lasts 12–13 minutes. I have to say, going there turned out to be a great decision. It taught me how to switch off my brain chatter, for at least some of the day, and I've found that it helps my creativity hugely.

Meditation is a tried-and-tested method for quietening brain chatter, but there are other methods that are equally effective, rooted in disciplines like psychology and neuroscience. Here are a few suggestions you can pick and choose from as needed, when your inner chatter gets particularly noisy.

COGNITIVE BEHAVIOUR THERAPY (CBT)

Cognitive behavioural therapy (CBT) is a form of talk therapy that can help you manage your problems by changing the way you think and behave. The research here is also pretty incontrovertible: CBT works. As with meditation, here you're also working to rewire the brain over time.

PRACTICE MINDFULNESS

Very close in style to mediation, mindfulness teaches you pay attention to the present rather than what's bouncing around in your head. The practice of mindfulness will pull your attention back to what you're doing at the moment, helping you focus on that alone.

EXERCISE

There's substantial evidence that physical exercise can help slow down your brain chatter, as well as being an all-round positive thing for your mental health. Walking briskly for 40 minutes will get boost your oxygen intake and get your pulse up, as will many other physical activities. The benefit of walking in particular is that you can combine it with mindfulness. As you walk, just try and stay in the moment, focusing only on what you can see, hear, smell or touch.

YOGA

There are a number of health benefits associated with practicing yoga. It is well documented that yoga helps reduce stress and anxiety and enhance one's overall sense of well-being. It will also help improve general physical fitness. Practicing yoga may lead to improved balance, flexibility, range of motion and strength. Combining yoga with mindfulness delivers great benefits, like calming your brain and giving you space to think.

The internet is full of scientific and medical resources to back up all these ideas. But you might want to talk to your doctor, or a trained counsellor or therapist, to zero in on which ones will suit you best.

And so, if you really want to be more creative, switch off the tech for some of the day, put down the newspaper, go into your bliss station and find the best techniques to quiet the chatter.

You will be amazed by the results.

THE TV MATRIX
INHIBITOR: TV

I have a confession to make: I love watching TV.

It might be a new BBC thriller, a Netflix drama, *MasterChef*, an Amazon Prime documentary, *Antiques Roadshow*, a Sky film or some sporting event. It is one of the ways I like to switch off and relax.

And according to a recent article in *The Times*, I am not alone. Technology correspondent Tom Knowles cited a report by Ofcom, the UK's broadcasting, telecoms and postal regulator, saying that British adults spent a third of their waking hours watching TV and online video content in 2020. That is an average of five hours and 40 minutes a day.

That total is 47 minutes more than the 2019 average, and amounts to about 2,500 hours over the course of the year. The article noted that by September 2020, 60% of homes in Britain were subscribing to a streaming service such as BBC iPlayer, Netflix or Prime Video.

For the younger generation, it must be hard to believe that as recently as 1982 Britain had only three television channels: BBC's 1 and 2, and ITV. Home video recording was still young — with big plastic videocassettes! — and although the satellite and cable revolution had been threatening to erupt for some time, the arrival of the first UK operators was still a few years off.

Fast forward to 2022, and the UK has a wide array of free-to-air, free-to-view and subscription services over a variety of distribution media, through which there are more than 480 channels for consumers, as well as an abundance of on-demand content.

Beyond the staggering number of channels that are available, there are also many more ways to watch television today: smart TVs, mobile phones, laptops and tablets. We can also record or watch programming on any number of catch-up channels.

There are many advantages to having all this choice.

First, television is an easy and cheap source of entertainment. At the same time, if we want to be kept informed on breaking news around the world, you have 24-hour news channels.

There are loads of useful do-it-yourself shows, giving us easy access to all kinds of information. For example, home improvement shows teach us how to do 'DIY' better, and financial advisers give pointers for managing finances and investing money. Cooking channels offer new recipes and methods, as well as a glimpse into some of the world's most famous restaurants.

TV can expand your mind. Travels shows provide insight into different people, cultures, cities and countries you'll never have an opportunity to visit in person. Documentaries provide us with a broader understanding of the world we live in and expose us to things we might not otherwise experience.

Television also helps us to be less lonely. Psychologists call this 'social surrogacy,' describing TV a surrogate for real interaction that can mimic the experience of belonging. A study published in *The Journal of Experimental Social Psychology* found that people who watch a favourite TV show report feeling less lonely during the programme.

Believe it or not, there may be certain physical health benefits to watching television as well. If a TV show makes you laugh, it's likely to make you more relaxed and improve your mood. One study from the University of Rochester found that people felt more energetic after watching nature scenes. While exercising, television can distract you from what you're doing, enabling you to last longer on the treadmill. (There's a good reason so many gyms have televisions after all!)

As you can see, there are advantages on many levels to watching TV. But, the key question is, does it inhibit creativity?

THE CREATIVITY DOWNSIDE

A fascinating article on the *Economic Times* website suggested that children who spend just 15 minutes watching television may become less creative, compared to those who read books or solve jigsaw puzzles. Contradictory study results from Staffordshire University found that watching TV for short periods does not impact the number of creative ideas young children come up with. However, that research, conducted with 60 three-year-olds, found that 15 minutes of children's television temporarily reduces the originality of the ideas they come up with.

Meanwhile, a large-scale study carried out in Canada in the 1980s showed that a child was able to be more creative by not watching TV. As television was gradually being extended across that country, the study compared children in three communities: one that had four TV channels, one with a single channel and one with no television at all.

The Canadian researchers studied these communities just before one of the towns obtained television for the first time, and again two years later. The kids in the no-TV town scored significantly higher than the others on divergent thinking skills, a measure of imaginativeness. This was until they, too, got TV, at which point their outside-the-box ideation skills dropped to the same level as that of the other children.

And there's compelling evidence that watching too much TV can be detrimental to your physical health. For instance, studies have shown that there is a correlation between watching television and obesity. Watching TV for more than three hours a day can also contribute to sleep difficulties and behaviour problems.

If you want to use television to teach somebody, you must first teach them how to use television.

Umberto Eco

Others argue that watching TV is a waste of time. After all, it fills the time a person might have spent doing important, enriching things, like socially interacting with other human beings, being physically active, discovering the great outdoors, using one's own imagination, or spending time engaged in hobbies, like art, music and reading.

All these negatives point to too much TV inhibiting your ability to be more creative. I've also realized that of all the chapters I have written in my books, only a couple of them were inspired by something I had watched on TV. In the main, I get my ideas from newspaper articles, books, podcasts, TED Talks and educational websites. So, maybe I have been watching too much of the wrong TV programmes.

But the fact remains that I love watching television. So, for me at least, it becomes a matter of striking a balance between enjoying TV and doing so in a way that doesn't dampen creativity.

UNBLOCK   REFRAMING YOUR RELATIONSHIP

Maybe we are looking at this the wrong way 'round. I'd suggest that it is not the amount of TV you watch, but instead the type of programmes. It's the same with websites and social apps, as well as the books and newspapers you digest. Some will inspire creative ideas, others will not.

Like anything in life, you need to strike the right balance between those programmes that will creatively inspire you and those that are really just a form of entertainment. Shows such as *Game of Thrones*, *Love Island*, *I'm a Celebrity, Get Me Out of Here!*,

Homeland and *Succession* obviously fall into the pure entertainment category.

They're probably not going to educate you, and won't really help you become more creative. But they are likely to relax you and help your brain switch off for a while. All of that is good.

However, I think things might get problematic if these are the only these types of shows you watch. If you're spending four to five hours a day staring at entertainment programming, that may not set off a creative explosion. As I have said, creativity is not a linearly thing with a structured process and a definite end. Rather, it can start anytime. All you need is that creative spark, and the innovative thinking begins. The problem is, if you spend your evenings watching only entertainment programming, where will the spark come from?

I want you to think of a typical day. Maybe you get out of bed and set off for work around 9 am. You have a demanding job, where there is little time for real creativity and innovation. At lunch, you pop out to the sandwich shop and chat with a colleague about something you heard on the news. Then, it's back to your desk for the rest of the afternoon. You get home around 6:15 pm and spend time with your children, finally getting them to bed around 7:30 pm.

You are physically and emotionally tired, and all you want to do is kick back, turn on the TV and watch your favourite escapist programmes. You switch off the set around 11:00 pm and go to bed... and the same routine starts again the next morning.

And therein lies the problem: where do you find the time to watch the kinds of programmes that could help you to be more creative? And, more importantly, what exactly are the types of shows you should try and watch more often?

Let's call these 'inspired TV programmes.' They might be entertaining, but they're also factual, educational or motivational. This is what you should be trying to watch more of, as they're more likely to inspire your creativity.

BOAST   INSPIRED TV PROGRAMMES

As mentioned, out of the dozens of chapters I have written over the years, only two were inspired by something I'd seen on TV. They definitely qualified as 'inspired.'

I will share the story about one of these chapters. It was called 'Identifying your goals,' in my 2019 book, *Positive Thinking*, where I looked to redefine the meaning of a positive mindset for the 21st century. I shared the story of a TV documentary called *Walking the Amazon*, which charted the explorer Ed Stafford's successful attempt to walk the length of the Amazon River. He started at its source in Peru and ended at the sea in northeastern Brazil. It took him two and a half years, and he endured more than 200,000 mosquito and ant bites, got 600 wasp stings and wore out six pairs of boots.

This feat of endurance had a big impact on me. Not only was the walk an extremely difficult physical challenge, but it was also an emotional rollercoaster. Along the way, Ed experienced not only bouts of despair, fear, exhaustion and sadness, but also joy, laughter, happiness and elation.

This remarkable journey was the reason I needed to write a chapter about having the right type of goals (which Ed had), and why they are key to thinking positively. That documentary inspired me so much, and it provided the creative thought to reference it, both here and in the previous book.

That is the just a small example of the power of watching inspiring TV programmes, which can help make you more creative.

To help you find this inspiration, I want you to try and compete a very simple matrix. You'll list the last seven days of TV shows you've watched, placing them in either the 'pure entertainment' or 'inspiration and entertainment' columns. I define 'pure entertainment' as those shows that you really enjoy, but aren't going to inspire you to be more creative in your life. Conversely, 'inspirational and entertainment' programming does just that.

YOUR TV MATRIX

PURE ENTERTAINMENT	INSPIRATIONAL AND ENTERTAINMENT

What you are trying to do is either reduce the amount of pure enter-tainment shows you view, and replace them with more inspirational and entertainment choices... or make more time to watch only in-spirational and entertainment programming. Basically, you need a balance of both.

Here is part of my matrix over the last seven days:

NEIL FRANCIS'S TV MATRIX

PURE ENTERTAINMENT	INSPIRATIONAL AND ENTERTAINMENT
NEED LESS	*NEED MORE*
SUCCESSION	*MASTERCHEF*
LOTS OF RUGBY UNION	
IMPEACHMENT	
THE LAKES WITH SIMON REEVE	
CLOSE TO ME	
HAVE I GOT NEWS FOR YOU	
THE WHITE LOTUS	
ANGELA BLACK	

As you can see, my current split is around 90:10, heavily weighted towards pure entertainment. And so, it's not surprising that I seldom get creative inspiration from TV. Maybe I need to take a leaf out of my own book and get my viewing habits into better balance.

I know that if you get that ratio right, it will only help you to be more creative, as this will be one of the places where you will get new ideas, insights and inspiration.

MORE 'STUFF,'
LESS CREATIVITY
INHIBITOR: STUFF

Don't ask me why, but years ago I became fascinated by the annual publication of the *World Happiness Report*. Prepared by the UN Sustainable Development Solutions Network, based on polling conducted by the Gallup organization, it reflects how happy people in 149 countries perceive themselves to be. It examines factors that impact happiness, and ranks cities and countries, from happiest to most miserable.

The report includes articles by experts in economics, psychology and other disciplines, who put the survey data into context and examine the objective benefits of happiness, the progress of nations, associated mental health issues and public policy implications.

The report uses six variables to measure the quality of life and resulting levels of happiness. These include: GDP per capita; social support; healthy life expectancy; freedom; generosity; and absence of corruption.

The 2020 report was published in March of 2021. It advised that if you want to live in the happiest country in the world, pack your bags and fly to Finland. For the third year running, Finland remains the happiest country in the world. If you've always dreamed of moving to Denmark, that Nordic nation ranked second. Or, if you're into skiing and fondue, move to Switzerland, which had the third-highest happiness rating. (At the dismal far end of the spectrum, Afghanistan was deemed the least happy country in the world in 2021.)

What I find interesting about the variables used in the study is that wealth or material goods are not included as a measurement of happiness. This is no surprise, as there is substantial evidence that there is no correlation between money, physical 'stuff' and personal happiness.

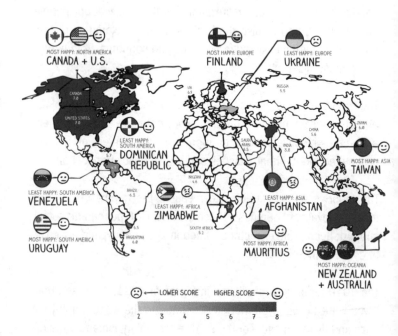

You'd be mistaken if you automatically assumed that billionaires, with their yachts, exotic holidays and luxury homes, are supremely happy. In 2006, Princeton University psychologist, economist and author Daniel Kahneman and a team of other academics published the results of a study titled, 'Would you be happier if you were richer? A focusing illusion.'

Kahneman's study challenged the assumption that wealth leads to happiness. The team found that although people with high incomes are more likely than others to say they're generally happy with their lives, this virtually disappears when they make a moment-to-moment assessment of how happy they really are.

But what is interesting about both the UN survey and the Princeton research is that many people worldwide still feel that success, and therefore happiness, is measured based by how much stuff you own.

A 2013 a study conducted by the global research firm IPSOS surveyed people from 20 countries to gauge the importance of material things *vis-à-vis* how successful one feels. The first question asked whether respondents agreed that 'I measure my success by the things I own.' The top three countries whose citizens said 'yes' were China (71%), India (58%) and Turkey (57%). The researchers then asked respondents if agreed that 'I feel under a lot of pressure to be successful and make money.' China was again had the most affirmative responses, with 68% saying yes. South Africa and Russia each had 66% of respondents saying that was the case.

Overall, the research seemed to indicate that there is a correlation between the stage of a country's development and its tendency to equate money with success. People residing in China, India and Brazil, three of the world's biggest developing countries, were among the likeliest to measure success by material belongings.

What I find particularly fascinating is that if you look at the positioning of these five countries on the World Happiness Report, you see the following: Brazil ranks 32nd; Russia 73rd; Turkey 93rd; China 94th; and India 144th. And so, the data clearly reflect that the more a country equates success with material possessions, the less happy its citizens actually are.

Going back to creative thinking, this all dovetails with a growing body of evidence showing that the more material goods you have, the less creative you become.

UNBLOCK   THE CONSTRAINT MINDSET

Intuitively, it might seem that the more resources we have available to us, the more tools and opportunities we have to stretch our creative wings. Not so, according to the results of a 2015 study that associated scarcity, not abundance, with greater creativity.

Researchers from Johns Hopkins University's Carey Business School and the University of Illinois conducted six experiments to test the affects of having more, versus having less, on creativity. The study described a "constraint mindset" — a mode of thinking activated by having less. The greater the constraint mindset, it seems, the more creatively a person will make use of his or her limited resources. Their findings indicate that necessity is indeed the mother of invention.

"New inventions and innovations – they all come from creativity. So how does an abundance mindset affect creativity?" said Ravi Mehta, a Professor of Business Administration at the University of Illinois and lead study author. "What we found is that abundant resources may have a negative effect on creativity. When you have fewer resources, you use them more creatively."

The researchers were specifically looking at how consumers make use of products when they have more or fewer resources available to them. In our product-saturated economy, we have little incentive to creatively maximize what's available, an outcome that makes even more sense when you compare affluent and poor countries.

"If you look at people who don't have resources or only have limited resources, they actually end up being more creative with what they have," said Mehta. "If you go to a poor country and see how they solve problems by repurposing older products, it's super-innovative."

With instant digital gratification available to us at any moment of the day or night, what role does creative inspiration play? When younger generations have prefabricated imagination on tap, from video games and smartphones, where's the need for creating something newly imagined?

FOCUSING ILLUSION

The Princeton study referenced above, published in *Science* magazine, noted that when people are encouraged to consider the affect
of a single factor on their well-being — in this case, money — they're
prone to exaggerate its importance. Kahneman and his colleagues
found that standard survey questions, such as those used in the
UN's *World Happiness Report*, may induce a phenomenon they call
the "focusing illusion." In this instance, it would draw people's attention to their relative affluence.

As such, survey respondents are in effect misled into believing
that more money can, and does, make them happier. When you
strip away the distorting lens of this focusing illusion, I would argue that the more you dwell on material goods, the *less happy* you
actually become.

The same principles apply to creativity. By focusing on the acquisition of material goods — for example, if you spend lots of time re-
searching and which new car you should buy — you have little time
or energy to think creatively. When you then immediately pivot to
obsessing over those cool mesh-woven trainers everybody's wearing, and the expensive Japanese kitchen knife you saw on TV, and
that fabulous vintage guitar on eBay, your focus is consumed by
material wants. You assign each of these physical things inordinate
significance, one after another, which has the effect of neutralizing
any creative, blue-sky impulses.

In Chapter 4, we talked about creativity not having linear flow, unlike
many of the mundane daily tasks you undertake. When you enter
into an unstructured, free-flowing creative state, you may spend
long periods of time reading, contemplating, sketching out ideas,

and loosely trying out possible solutions. You might feel like you aren't making any clear progress towards your goal, but down deep, the subconscious gears are turning. And then, it happens: you hit on a really great idea, and suddenly have the sense that a solution may be in sight.

On the other hand, the focusing illusion does have a linear flow. You focus on that next material purchase and spend a lot of time thinking about it. That will then be a significant inhibitor to creativity, which will in turn make you less innovative in addressing the challenges and possibilities you're presented with.

How can we stop this illusory obsession from inhibiting our creativity? Well, it's time to go for a walk.

BOOST   TIME FOR A WALK

I'd suggest that one of the best ways to avoid the trap of the focusing illusion is to spend more time with Mother Nature.

My favourite things in life don't cost any money. It's really clear that the most precious resource we all have is time.

Steve Jobs

Here are four ways that researchers say this can help inspire creativity:

1. Nature Can Help You Get Inspired

A Stanford University study found that when people spend time in the great outdoors, many experience a shift in how they view time itself. They can be awestruck by the wonders of the natural world, and get a sense that time is expanding. Instead of feeling pressured by thoughts about material things, they can experience 'time abundance,' and a sense of being unencumbered, with their thoughts freely flowing in lots of different directions.

2. Nature Can Help You Overcome Creative Blocks

As we've discussed, if you are thinking constantly about which 52-inch plasma TV you should purchase, it's easy to get bogged down with a creative block. The good news is that quality time outdoors can help you overcome that impediment.

A 2012 study conducted by psychologists from the University of Utah and the University of Kansas found that spending quality time outside improved peoples' Remote Associates Test (RAT) results.

This test, developed in the late 1950s, purports to measure creative potential using word-association. Subjects are given three seemingly unrelated 'stimulus words' and asked to come up with a fourth word that ties the others together in a meaningful way, Test-takers who exhibit 'convergent thinking' — the ability to reach one well-defined solution to a problem — are deemed creatively gifted.

For purposes of this study, the test was given to 56 participants going on a four-day hiking trip. The researchers had 24 participants take the test before they began their excursion, while the other 32 took it on the fourth day of the hike. Remarkably, the results showed that that four days in nature helped participants improve their RAT scores by 50%.

3. Nature Increases Brain Function
Focusing on material thoughts for a lot of the day can be tiring and stressful. For the brain to function at its highest possible level, you need to be able to reduce fatigue and boost your energy levels.

This allows your brain to restore itself, so you can start thinking of new ideas and solutions to problems you might be facing. A 2009 study jointly conducted by researchers in the US, Germany and Canada, published in the *Journal of Environmental Psychology*, concluded that 20 minutes a day outside is all you may need to allow your brain to refresh, restore and start functioning optimally again.

4. It Improves Your Mental Health
If you are focusing on material goods, chances are you will become more stressed and anxious, which might be a sign that you are struggling with your mental health. In that agitated state, you'll never be able to reach your full creative potential. Spending time in nature can help boost your mood and improve your overall mental well-being.

A 2021 study conducted by the UK mental health charity Mind involved participants who either went for a walk in nature or a walk through a shopping mall. The researchers found that 71% of those who took a nature walk had reduced symptoms of depression. As for the mall-walkers, 22% were actually more depressed afterward.

Next time you're tempted to start thinking about that next material purchase you feel you really want, consider heading for the woods, a park or the beach instead. You'll be amazed how much more creative you will feel.

Be who you are and say what you feel, because those who mind don't matter and those who matter don't mind.

Dr Seuss

PART THREE

IT STARTS
AND ENDS
WITH YOU

THE SPARK
IN YOUR IMAGINATION

The following four brilliant achievements are seemingly unrelated, but there is a tie that binds them. Read on, and see if you can guess what they have in common.

Neptune's Staircase. In the small Scottish village of Banavie, in the shadow of Ben Nevis, the tallest mountain in the British Isles, is the remarkable Neptune's Staircase. An amazing feat of engineering, this quarter-mile chain of eight locks incrementally raises a commercial shipping canal by 19 metres (62 feet). Built by civil engineer Thomas Telford between 1803 and 1822, it is the longest staircase lock in Scotland.

The Camera. George Eastman pioneered mass-market photography in the late 19th century when he started producing paper film. He patented his first rolled film in 1884 and perfected the first camera using it in 1888. That same year, George introduced the Kodak camera into the market. It was a unique box camera that came with a film roll big enough for 100 photos.

The Life Raft. In 1882, US inventor Maria Beasely decided that people should stop dying at sea. We've been navigating the seas for millennia, but the primitive lifeboats that existed at the time were not an effective solution in the event of a SOS situation. Thanks to Maria, whose patented creation featured collapsible floats in airtight containers, thousands of lives have been saved, including an estimated 706 when the Titanic sank. (She also in-vented a foot-warmer, barrel-hooping machine, anti-derailment device for trains and a dozen other patented innovations.)

The Ice Cream Maker. In 1846, Nancy Johnson patented a de-sign for a hand-operated ice cream maker that made it possible for anyone to create that frozen confection. Nancy's device com-prised two perforated spatulas, attached to a shaft rotated by a crank and tightly fitted into a long cylindrical barrel. The outside of the cylinder was cooled with a mixture of salt and ice. Nancy's invention is still used to this day, from small kitchen models to those in factories producing ice cream on a large scale.

So, what connects these four achievements? The answer is that they all started in the creator's imagination. Everything in your home, or at your place of work, was either invented, or improved upon, by individuals using their imagination. At some point, a cre-ative spark ignited, leading to so many priceless innovations.

"

Imagination does not become great until human beings, given the courage and the strength, use it to create.

"

Maria Montessori

It is through creative thinking that we have solved some of history's most vexing scientific, medical, engineering and technological problems. We've found clever solutions that have immeasurably improved peoples' lives around the world. That is the power and the importance of creative thinking.

Hopefully, I have shown in this book that the key to successful creative thinking is to understand and stop the inhibitors that can block your progress. It's there for you to tap into, whoever you are, because I fundamentally believe creativity is in everyone's DNA, soul and nature.

I have tried to share ideas, thoughts and insights that will fire up your imagination, leading to sparks of creativity that will revolutionize your life in so many positive ways. But don't stop here. You don't have to constantly search for ways to fuel your imagination... you simply need to be more curious and seek to increase your knowledge.

You see, without extending our knowledge, our ability to see things not as they are, but *as they might be*, is greatly hindered. If you cannot imagine new possibilities, or seek out new opportunities based on your current knowledge, your ability to think creatively will be stunted. How can you think of innovative new ways to pen a book, solve a work challenge, write a song or set up a new business if you keep coming back to tired old ideas?

Strive to increase your knowledge, every single day. Reading is obviously key, whether you turn to books, newspapers, blogs, tweets, websites, Instagram, LinkedIn and Facebook posts – all will increase your knowledge. And rather than following things you're currently interested in, try delving into areas that will challenge your conventional thinking. One tweet or post about something new could be the catalyst that sparks your imagination.

If reading is not your thing, then watch TED Talks, webcasts, documentaries and films, or listen to podcasts, radio programmes or audiobooks. Go to art galleries, museums, book festivals, bookshops, conferences, lectures and public seminars to get new ideas and perspectives.

By doing this, you will challenge your existing thinking, so that when you're presented with a new opportunity you will not automatically revert back to what you already know. Your mind will go in the direction of a more creative solution. If you can increase your knowledge on new subjects or further challenges, your imagination is more likely to flourish.

I think that one of the most important benefits of being a more curious person is that you will become open-minded to new ideas and interests. And this is when your imagination can really get to work!

Study the lives of some of the world's greatest innovators, entrepreneurs, explorers, engineers, scientists, medics and artists, and you will see that being curious is one of the key ingredients that made them really creative. Alexander Fleming, Rosalind Franklin, Pablo Picasso, Marie Curie, Leonardo da Vinci, Tracey Emin, Neil Armstrong and Florence Nightingale would have all been motivated to continuously increase their knowledge. With this new insight and understanding, they were then able to create wonderful art, solve medical challenges and even walk on the moon!

Whenever you feel your potential to become more creative is being blocked by the inhibitors in your life, remember the ideas, tips and strategies I have given you to calm down, unblock, open up and boost your imagination. Firing up your curiosity will allow your imagination to be the spark that ignites your creativity, leading you to exciting, innovative new ideas ready to be put into action.

Hopefully, all of this will make you even more passionate about creativity, which will prove infectious to everyone around you.

And then, as Albert Einstein said, "Creativity is contagious. Pass it on!"

REFERENCES
AND RESOURCES

DNA

Gavius Apicius, Marcus, *The De Re Coquinaria* – New Edition (Dover Publications, Inc; Mineola, New York, 1978).

Galton, Francis, '*Hereditary Genius*,' last modified 2016. https://en.wikipedia.org/wiki/Hereditary_Genius

Cox, David, 'Are some people born creative?,' *Guardian*, 19 September 2013. https://www.theguardian.com/science/blog/2013/sep/19/born-creative-study-brain-hemingway

Taramas, Kittisak, Getty Images.

NATURE

Lents, Nathan, 'Why do humans make art?,' last modified 5 September 2017. https://www.psychologytoday.com/za/blog/beastly-behavior/201709/why-do-humans-make-art

SOUL

History.com editors, 'Printing press,' last modified 10th October, 2019. https://www.history.com/topics/inventions/printing-press

Twain, Mark, *Autobiography of Mark Twain*, (University of California Press, Reader's edition, Oakland, California, 7 February 2012).

'The history of innovation cycles,' Visual Capitalist, Image.

Gallagher, James, 'Oxford vaccine: how did they make it so quickly?,' *BBC News*, 23 October 2020. https://www.bbc.co.uk/news/health-55041371

Adobe Systems, Inc, 'Study Reveals Global Creativity Gap,' 23 April 2012. https://news.adobe.com/news/news-details/2012/Study-Reveals-Global-Creativity-Gap/default.aspx

EDUCATION

Brown, Deborah; Quinn, Kelly; Brierley, Jenny, 'Dear Year 6 pupils,' *ITV This Morning*, 8 May 2015. https://bit.ly/3aAMvjM

Robinson, Ken, 'Do schools kill creativity?,' TED Talk, February 2006. https://www.ted.com/talks/sir_ken_robinson_do_schools_kill_creativity?language=en

Minchin, Tim, '9 life lessons,' University of Western Australia Commencement Address, 25 September 2013. http://www.timminchin.com/2013/09/25/occasional-address

WORK

Martin, Colette; Hedges, Kristi, 'Creativity is the new black,' *Forbes*, 16 July 2010. https://www.forbes.com/sites/work-in-progress/2010/07/16/creativity-is-the-new-black/?sh=42169eaa62df

Clark, Pilita, 'How the modern office is killing our creativity,' *Financial Times*, 15 March 2019. https://www.ft.com/content/6148ec14-457a-11e9-a965-23d669740bfb

'Ringelmann Effect,' *Psychology*, last accessed May 2022. http://psychology.iresearchnet.com/social-psychology/group/ringelmann-effect/

Asok, Deepu, 'Social Loafing,' Image.

NEWS

Dobelli, Rolf, *Stop Reading the News: A Manifesto for a Happier, Calmer and Wiser Life* (Sceptre; London, England, 2020).

Heid, Markham, 'You asked: Is it bad for you to read the news constantly?,' *Time*, 19 May 2020. https://time.com/5125894/is-reading-news-bad-for-you/

Graziano Beruning, Loretta, *Habits of a Happy Brain – Retrain your Brain to Boost Your Serotonin, Dopamine, Oxytocin & Endorphin Levels* (Adams Media; Adams, Massachusettes, December 2015).

CONCRETE

Kinver, Mark, 'Millions "lack access" to parks and green spaces,' *BBC News*, 27 May 2019.
https://www.bbc.co.uk/news/science-environment-48398033

Li, Qing, 'Shinrin-yoku, the art and science of forest-bathing', TFBI, last accessed May 2022. https://tfb.institute/scientific-research/

STEREOTYPES

Siltanen, Rob, 'The real story behind Apple's "Think Different" campaign', *Forbes*, 14 December 2011. https://bit.ly/37xPeJ6

'Redraw the balance', Inspiring The Future, March 2016. https://www.inspiringthefuture.org/inspiring-women/ redraw-the-balance/

Gino, Francesca, *Rebel Talent: Why It Pays To Break The Rules At Work And In Life* (Dey Street Books; New York, New York, May 2018). https://francescagino.com/books

TECH

Kleon, Austin, *Keep Going: 10 Ways To Stay Creative In Good Times And Bad* (Workman Publishing Company; New York, New York, April 2019).

Alexsandr, Mansurov, Dreamtime.com, Image.

Tew, Alex; Smith, Michael, 'The Calm App.' https://www.calm.com/

TV

Butler, Fionnuala; Pickett, Cynthia, 'Imaginary friends: Television programs can fend off loneliness', *Scientific American*, 28 July 2009. https://www.scientificamerican.com/article/imaginary-friends/

Ryan, Richard; Weinstein, Netta; Bernstein, Jessey; Warren Brown, Kirk; Mistretta, Louis; Gagne, Marylene, 'Spending time in nature makes people more alive, study shows,' *Science Daily*, 3 June 2010. https://www.rochester.edu/news/show.php?id=3639

STUFF
Helliwell, John; Layard, Richard; Sachs, Jeffrey; De Neve, Jan-Emmanuel; Aknin, Lara; Wang, Shun, *World Happiness Report 2021*, last accessed May 2022.
https://worldhappiness.report/ed/2021/

'The most and least happy countries around the world,' Visual Capitalist, Image.

Kahneman, Daniel; Kruger, Alan; Schkade, David; Schwarz, Norbert; Stone, Arthur, 'Would you be happier if you were richer? A focusing illusion,' Princeton University Center for Economic Policy Studies, May 2006. https://bit.ly/2RvP2EA

'Global attitudes on materialism, finances and family,' IPSOS Group SA, December 2013.
https://www.ipsos.com/sites/default/files/news_and_polls/2013-12/6359.pdf

DiSalvo, David, 'The more stuff we have, the less creative we are,' *Forbes*, 19 November 2015.
https://www.forbes.com/sites/daviddisalvo/2015/11/19/study-the-more-stuff-we-have-the-less-creative-we-are/?sh=3a86ea1c505c

Goodstein, Eli, 'Stanford University study says spending time in nature benefits mental health,' *USA Today*, 9 July 2015. https://eu.usatoday.com/story/college/2015/07/09/stanford-university-study-says-spending-time-in-nature-benefits-mental-health/37404415/

'Nature nurtures creativity,' The University of Utah, 12 December 2012. https://archive.unews.utah.edu/news_releases/nature-nurtures-creativity-2/

'Spending time in nature makes people feel more alive, study shows,' *Science Daily*, 4 June 2010. https://www.sciencedaily.com/releases/2010/06/100603172219.htm

ABOUT THE AUTHOR

NEIL FRANCIS is the co-founder and Executive Chairman of Pogo Studio, a digital consulting and solutions agency based in Edinburgh, Scotland. He is the author of *The Creative Thinking Book*, *Inspired Thinking*, *Positive Thinking*, *The Entrepreneur's Book* and *Changing Course*. His books have been translated into multiple foreign languages, including Chinese.

In 2006, at the age of 41, Neil suffered a stroke, which eventually led him to discover a new, more meaningful and rewarding life. This now includes working with inspiring CEOs, leaders, charity bosses and entrepreneurs, while continuing to work as an author and as head of a successful web and mobile technology firm.

He lives in North Berwick, Scotland, with his wife and two daft Golden Retrievers.

www.neil-francis.com
www.pogo-studio.com
neil@neil-francis.com

BY THE SAME AUTHOR

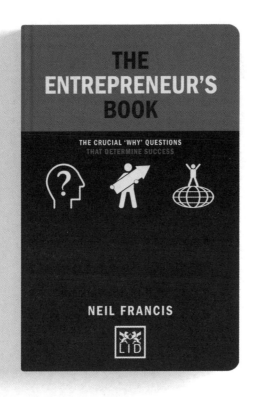

£9.99/$14.95
ISBN: 978-1-911498-81-0

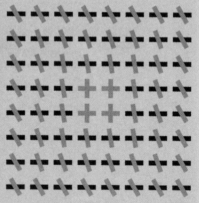

POSITIVE
THINKING

NEIL FRANCIS

HOW TO CREATE A WORLD
FULL OF POSSIBILITIES

£9.99/$14.95
ISBN:978-1-912555-15-4

INSPIRED THINKING

NEIL FRANCIS

HOW TO DISCOVER NEW IDEAS
FOR MEANINGFUL SUCCESS

LID

£9.99/$14.95
ISBN: 978-1-912555-77-2